NOBODY LEFT TO HATE
Teaching Compassion After Columbine

Books by Elliot Aronson

Handbook of Social Psychology (with G. Lindzey)

Theories of Cognitive Consistency (with R. Abelson)

Voices of Modern Psychology

The Social Animal

Readings About The Social Animal

Social Psychology (with R. Helmreich)

Research Methods in Social Psychology
(with J. M. Carlsmith and P. Ellsworth)

The Jigsaw Classroom

Burnout: From Tedium to Personal Growth
(with A. Pines and D. Kafry)

Energy Use: The Human Dimension (with P. C. Stern)

The Handbook of Social Psychology (with G. Lindzey)

Career Burnout (with A. Pines)

Methods of Research in Social Psychology
(with P. Ellsworth, J. M. Carlsmith, and R. Gonzales)

Age of Propaganda (with A. R. Pratkanis)

Social Psychology, Volumes 1, 2, and 3
(with A. R. Pratkanis)

Social Psychology: The Heart and the Mind
(with T. Wilson and R. Akert)

Cooperation in the Classroom: The Jigsaw Method
(with S. Patnoe)

NOBODY LEFT TO HATE
Teaching Compassion After Columbine

Elliot Aronson

University of California at Santa Cruz

A W. H. FREEMAN / OWL BOOK

Henry Holt and Company | New York

Henry Holt and Company, LLC
Publishers since 1866
115 West 18th Street
New York, New York 10011

Henry Holt® is a registered trademark of
Henry Holt and Company, LLC.

Library of Congress Card Number: 00-101462

Nobody Left to Hate: Teaching Compassion After Columbine
ISBN: 0-8050-7099-0 (pbk.)

Henry Holt books are available for special promotions and
premiums. For details contact: Director, Special Markets.

First Owl Books Edition 2001

A W. H. Freeman/Owl Book

Printed in the United States of America.

7   9   10   8   6

To my grandchildren, their teachers,
and all their schoolmates

CONTENTS

PREFACE

Like most Americans, I was horrified and depressed when I saw the massacre at Columbine High School and the anguish of students and their parents unfold before my eyes on CNN. Like some Americans, I was appalled at the naïve and feeble solutions proposed by our policy makers in the aftermath of that horrifying event: more security guards and metal detectors in our schools, forcing students to show respect for their teachers by calling them "sir" and "ma'am," and posting the Ten Commandments on school bulletin boards. I thought, "Surely our lawmakers can do better than that."

Then it dawned on me that I could do better than that. As a social psychologist who has worked in schools and helped create school environments where students learned to feel compassion and empathy for one another, I believe I have something useful to contribute to the national dialogue on this issue.

This book is the result of my thinking, during the past year, about the events of Columbine and what we might do to reduce the probability of such disasters in the future. In a very real sense, this book is actually the result of forty years of my thinking and scientific research aimed at trying to understand the intricacies of humans interacting with one another: How we come to like one another, hate one another, experience empathy for one another, and respect one another. From this research, I have described some effective interventions schools can make. The best part of it is that the interventions not only flow from decades of scientific research, they are also relatively easy and painless to put into operation.

Acknowledgments

Mine is the only name on the cover of this book. So, if you take issue with anything in it, I'm the guy you should holler at. But I never do anything important all by myself. This book is no exception. It pleases me to express my appreciation to my research assistant, Beverly McLeod, for her hard work and timely responses to my queries and demands.

In addition, I am blessed with an exciting and supportive family, all of whom patiently listen to my ideas, encourage the good ones, and argue with the not-so-good ones, enabling me to separate a few kernels of wheat from an awful lot of chaff. In the hectic final stages of writing and editing this book, a few family members went above and beyond the usual call of duty—so special thanks are due to Vera, Hal, and Julie Aronson and to Laura Stachel.

At the Worth/Freeman end of things I want to thank Catherine Woods, Tracey Kuehn, Sarah Segal, Barbara Rusin, Michael Kimball, Sloane Lederer, Laura Quinn, Jeff Theis, Theresa Danks, Sheridan Sellers, and Fernando Quiñones for their creativity and hard work to get this book out in a timely manner.

1

WHAT HAPPENED AT COLUMBINE?

It was April 20, 1999, the day that the corridors, the classrooms, and the library of Columbine High School reverberated with the sound of gunshots. Two students, consumed by rage and armed with an arsenal of guns and explosives, went on a rampage, killing a teacher and several of their fellow students. They then turned their guns on themselves. After the shooting stopped, the building was eventually secured by a SWAT team. They found fifteen people dead (including the two shooters) and twenty-three more who needed to be hospitalized—some with severe wounds. It was the worst school massacre in our nation's history.

As horrendous as it was, we now know that the carnage could have been much worse. The two shooters made videotapes a few weeks before their massacre, and from these we have learned that they had carefully planned the event several months in advance. They actually prepared ninety-five explosive devices that failed to go off because of a simple electronic failure. Of these, one set, placed a few miles from the school, was intended to explode first and distract police by keeping them busy away from the school; a second set was supposed to go off in the cafeteria killing a great many students there and causing hundreds more to evacuate the building, in terror, where Eric Harris and Dylan Klebold would be waiting to gun them down; a third set was planted in their cars in the school parking lot, these timed to explode after the police and paramedics had arrived on the scene, creating more chaos and increasing the number of casualties. The videotapes show the two perpetrators gleefully predicting that, before the day was over, they would kill 250 people.

Try to imagine that you were the parent of a student at Columbine High School. That morning you lovingly packed a lunch for your daughter and sent her off to school before going about your own business. You were content in the belief that her high school was a safe and secure place. So there you are—listening to music on the radio while in your office, writing a memo to the boss, or driving home from the supermarket—when suddenly the music is interrupted by a news bulletin. The somber and somewhat rattled reporter makes the following announcement: "There has been a shooting at Columbine High School. Several students appear to have been killed or seriously wounded. Police have surrounded the school but have not yet entered. The gunmen are roaming free, armed with automatic weapons and explosives. Some students have managed to escape unharmed but most are still trapped in the school at the mercy of the gunmen."

I have four children and five grandchildren, all of whom have gone or will go to public school in various sections of this country. I know how I would feel. I can empathize with the shock and panic that undoubtedly gripped the parents of the Columbine students. I share the feelings of helplessness, despair, and anger that most parents and grandparents must have felt while watching the horrifying events unfold on the network news that evening or reading about them in the newspapers the next morning. Until recently, most residents of small towns and suburbs believed that extreme acts of violence were an unfortunate and tragic aspect of day-to-day life in the inner city, but that such things did not happen in affluent suburbs and small towns. The realization hit most parents like a punch in the stomach: If such a thing could happen in the middle-class community of Littleton, Colorado, it could happen anywhere. And, unfortunately, it *does* seem to be happening anywhere and everywhere—small towns and little cities that conjure up Norman Rockwell paintings: Littleton, Colorado; Conyers, Georgia; Notus, Idaho; Springfield, Oregon; Fayetteville, Tennessee; Edinboro, Pennsylvania; Jonesboro, Arkansas; West Paducah, Kentucky; Pearl, Mississippi; Fort Gibson, Oklahoma.

Ironically, these tragedies come at a time when violence, in general, and school violence, in particular, have been declining. In the past ten years, the annual number of school shootings has actually decreased. Broadly speaking, our schools are safe places. Indeed, for those youngsters who live in the crime-ridden, war zone neighborhoods of some of our most troubled inner cities—places like Detroit, New York, Los Angeles, Philadelphia, and Houston—their schools have become the safest place for them to be. Consider the data: There are approximately 50 million students attending some 108,000 public schools in this country, but fewer than one percent of adolescent homicides occur in or around schools.

So why all the panic? Shouldn't the media pundits be celebrating rather than wringing their hands in despair? Is all the attention being devoted to gun control and the safety of schools just another instance of the media taking a single tragic event and blowing it way out of proportion—manufacturing "trends" and "implications" where none exist?

I don't think so. Let's take a closer look. Yes, there has been a decline in the overall number of homicides in our schools. But this decline is almost certainly due to the fact that school officials in dangerous areas have installed metal detectors, surveillance cameras, and security guards in a prudent (and largely successful) attempt to prevent particularly violent or troubled youngsters from bringing weapons into the school.

The sobering statistic is that the number of incidents involving the killing of *multiple* victims in and around schools has risen sharply in the past few years. In less than two years, there have been eight multiple shootings of students by students, each of these in a place far removed from the turmoil of the inner city. A recent CBS/NY Times poll shows that fifty-two percent of teenagers from relatively benign communities now live with the fear that a Columbine-style attack could strike their school. And it is not only the students living with that fear; their parents also show a great deal of stress and anxiety around the issue of school safety.

WHAT TO DO?

In the sad aftermath of a school shooting—especially one as horrifying as the Columbine massacre, our first impulse is to blame someone. We demand to know who might have been negligent, who might have conspired with the killers, who should have seen the handwriting on the wall. We are not content with the explanation that this was performed by two disturbed youngsters. We want to look beyond them for the "real" culprit:

- Were the teachers or the principal negligent? Why didn't they spot trouble before it erupted?

- What about the parents of the shooters? How could reasonable parents not be aware that their sons kept guns in their bedrooms and were manufacturing pipe bombs in their garage?

- What's wrong with our schools, anyway? Why aren't they teaching our kids the difference between right and wrong?

- And aren't those video games and slasher movies making our youngsters more insensitive to the pain and suffering of real people—and to the permanence of death? If we could ban these forms of entertainment, wouldn't that make our schools safe again?

The need to blame is fully understandable. But if we truly want to address the problem, if we truly want to prevent future tragedies of this kind, then it is vital to make a clear distinction between two kinds of blaming: 1. The blaming that is aimed at finding the cause of the disaster so that we might come up with a workable intervention; 2. The blaming that is mere condemnation. Condemnation is a great indoor sport. It somehow makes us feel less helpless if we can unmask a culprit whom we can then proceed to vilify. If we decide that the culprit is a school administration that was asleep at the switch, then we can demand that the school principal be fired. But firing a principal will not solve the problem. If we decide the culprit was lax parenting, then perhaps we can humiliate or sue the parents of the killers. But humiliating and suing the killers' parents will not solve the problem either. This kind of blaming is a simple knee-jerk response. It won't do us much good in the long run.

But a lot of good can come from rational problem solving. And we humans *are* problem-solving animals. When a tragedy occurs, we want to know why. This is not idle curiosity. If we can pinpoint a cause, then we can fix it. For example, whenever an airliner crashes, a great deal of time and effort is expended to try to find the black box even if it's lying under 250 feet of turbulent ocean water. The black box becomes the focal point of a full-scale investigation: Was there a faulty design? Was there metal fatigue or a frayed electrical wire that had been overlooked in the previous inspection? Was it pilot error? Had ice been allowed to form on the wings of the plane while it waited on the runway? Was the plane carrying dangerous cargo? Could it have been a deliberate act of sabotage? The investigation is slow and painstaking. It typically requires several months or even years to complete.

In the aftermath of a school shooting, we are not inclined to be patient. We are tempted to look for instant solutions before we fully understand the cause of the problem. This is why Congress voted to tack on an amendment to the crime bill following the Columbine massacre. The amendment gives states the right to allow the display of the Ten Commandments in schools. "I understand that simply posting the Ten Commandments will not instantly change the moral character of our nation," said Robert Aderholt, the measure's sponsor. "However, it is an important step to

promote morality and an end of children killing children."
Ah, if it were only that simple!

Understandably, parents demanded more security and
many school officials were quick to comply. Schools across
the country have rushed to install metal detectors and
surveillance cameras. They have instituted ID policies. They
have ripped out lockers and required students to carry see-
through backpacks. They have also asked students to report
other students who threaten violence or who even seem different (dress strangely, keep to themselves, and so on). Some
schools have required that personality tests be administered to all students—tests aimed at profiling those students
who might be most apt to go on a murderous rampage.
Local police departments have conducted SWAT training at
high schools.

Newspaper columnists, TV pundits, politicians, and the
general public have been quick to blame permissive parents, lax school officials, the media, and society as a whole.
Self-proclaimed experts abound. Each seems to have a different idea of cause and cure. Those most prominently
mentioned appear in the box on page 9.

APPROACHING THE PROBLEM SCIENTIFICALLY

We need to look beyond the perpetrators if we want to
reduce the number of school massacres in the future. If
we simply dismissed the recent spate of multiple shootings at schools as the random acts of a handful of disturbed

POLITICALLY EXPEDIENT INTERVENTIONS

Problems	Quick-Fix Solutions
Not enough moral training in our educational institutions?	Allow prayer in schools or post the Ten Commandments in every classroom.
Too much violent imagery in the media?	Clamp down on violent movies, TV, and video games.
Too many guns, too easily available?	Institute more stringent gun control.
Youngsters are not respectful enough?	Make rules forcing them to call teachers "sir" and "ma'am."
Some students act different from what is considered the norm?	Identify them and either keep them under surveillance, remove them from the school, or subject them to intensive therapy until they are able to be like everybody else.

youngsters, we would be making a grave mistake. At the same time, it is important to look beyond the perpetrators in a meaningful way—with reasonable tools for looking. Before we rush in with an intervention, we must understand the deepest origins of the problem and the consequences of each proposed intervention.

Basically, there are two classes of intervention: root cause interventions and peripheral interventions. In my judgment, some of the so-called "cures" outlined in the box on page 9 have merit; others are useless; still others are almost certain to cause more harm than good. But they are all peripheral interventions. None of them—not even the useful ones—succeed in getting to the root of the problem. If a peripheral intervention (like gun control or metal detectors, for example) proves to be useful, there is no reason why it cannot be utilized. But we must realize that the deeper underlying problem will remain. And before we implement any kind of intervention, we must make sure that there is evidence supporting its use. What is immediately apparent is that most of these "cures" are not based on solid evidence—but rest on emotion, wishful thinking, bias, and political expediency.

Why do I say this? As a social psychologist, I have spent more than forty years studying how we humans behave and what motivates us to behave as we do. Social psychology is a science that is concerned with important aspects of human social behavior: persuasion, conformity, love, hate, aggression, prejudice, and the like—the stuff of human beings relating with one another. When I say I've been "studying" these things, I don't mean that I've simply been observing human behavior and speculating about what might have caused it. I mean that I have used these observations to specify concrete hypotheses, and then have tested these hypotheses in a rigorous scientific manner.

It might come as a surprise to most readers, but experimental social psychologists use strategies and techniques that are functionally identical to those used by medical researchers testing a new drug. Medical researchers would be drummed out of the business if they allowed themselves to rely entirely on idle speculation, bias, hearsay, folk wisdom, or political expediency to determine whether this or that drug might be helpful, harmful, or of no consequence. Moreover, medical researchers have learned that they cannot simply rely on the testimonials of patients who say they feel better after taking a new drug. After ingesting sugar pills or snake oil, many people feel better and some even think they are cured of serious illness. This is the well-known "placebo effect." The positive feelings generated by a placebo are of limited and temporary value. Yet there are still plenty of people around—some well-intentioned, others charlatans—who capitalize on the placebo effect by peddling untested substances as magical cures for a variety of conditions from acne to cancer. Fortunately, most consumers are now sophisticated enough to avoid spending huge sums of money on untested cures; most of us now require rigorous scientific investigation before we will ingest any old drug or concoction touted to cure a serious illness.

Such standards should be no less important in designing policies to influence human behavior—especially when the behavior in question is dysfunctional or destructive. For, in the absence of careful scientific investigation, we are just as apt to be fooled by our so-called "commonsense" notions of human nature as by a convincing huckster of snake oil. The fact is that commonsense notions of human behavior are frequently wrong and the consequences can be tragic. For example, from 1896 to 1954, most policy makers, as well as the general public, believed in the doctrine of "separate but equal." They believed that it did no harm to separate African-American schoolchildren from their white counterparts as long as the facilities were roughly equivalent. In 1954, social psychologists helped reverse this "commonsense" policy; they used scientific evidence to convince the Supreme Court that the mere fact of being segregated has a strong and negative impact on the self-esteem of minority youngsters that interferes with their ability to learn and can permanently stunt their intellectual and emotional development. In short, separate but equal is an oxymoron; being segregated, in and of itself, produces inequality.

So what wisdom does scientific social psychology have to offer concerning tragedies like Columbine and how to prevent them? Quite a lot. In the next several chapters, we will look at the speculations and cures mentioned in the box on page 9 through the lens of careful scientific studies. In doing so, we hope to separate the wheat of well-founded knowledge from the chaff of idle speculation on such topics as the easy availability of guns and the impact of media violence on the behavior of children and adolescents. We will also look at data pertinent to such interventions as the posting of the Ten Commandments and requiring students to say "sir" and "ma'am" when addressing their teachers. Most important, we will try to get to the root of the problem: We will scrutinize the social atmosphere prevalent in most high schools in this country and try to determine how this atmosphere might have contributed to the tragedies that unfolded in the classrooms of Littleton, West Paducah, Springfield, and other communities in recent years.

This last point requires some elaboration. There is no doubt in my mind that these violent acts were pathological. The perpetrators of these horrifying deeds were disturbed. Their behavior was beyond all reason. But if we chalk up these events *simply* to individual pathology and nothing else, then we are bound to miss something of vital importance. Based on my experience in schools throughout the nation, I would suggest that it is highly likely that the perpetrators were reacting in an extreme and pathological manner to a general atmosphere of exclusion. This is a school atmosphere that most of the student body finds unpleasant, distasteful, difficult, and even humiliating. If this is the case, then instituting a significant change in the social atmosphere of the classroom might succeed in making the school a safer place (reducing the possibility that students will become so disgruntled that they go over the edge and commit acts of extreme violence). This might also succeed in producing the kind of social environment that will make the school a more pleasant, more stimulating, more compassionate, and more humane place for all of the students. This is our ultimate goal.

WHY IT'S IMPORTANT TO AVOID JUMPING TO THE WRONG CONCLUSION

Why do we need to go about this scientifically or cautiously? Given the extreme importance of the problem, what's wrong with a scattershot strategy—trying several possible interventions at once—in the hope that one or more will do some good? As I implied earlier, the problem is that it is highly likely that some apparently sensible interventions could produce negative or even disastrous consequences, depending on what is actually going on in the school. Let me give you one cogent example. A few days after the Columbine tragedy, my 16-year-old grandson came home from high school and said, "Guess what? The principal sent around a notice asking us to report any kids who are dressing strangely, behaving weirdly, appear to be loners, or out of it."

At first glance, this might seem like a reasonable course of action: The authorities merely want to identify the kids who seem to fit the description of the Columbine shooters—kids who might be unbalanced or might cause trouble, kids who seem unpopular or separated from the other students, kids who dress in black trenchcoats or in other strange ways. The authorities can then keep an eye on them, offer them special counseling, or whatever. But my best guess is that the principal is shining his spotlight on the wrong part of the equation. Here's why: From my classroom research, I have found that the social atmosphere in most schools is competitive, cliquish, and exclusionary. The majority of teenagers I have interviewed agonize over the fact that there is a general atmosphere of taunting and rejection among their peers that makes the high school experience an unpleasant one. For many, it is worse than unpleasant—they describe it as a living hell, where they are in the out-group and feel insecure, unpopular, put-down, and picked on. By asking the "normal" students to point out the "strange" ones, my grandson's high school principal is unwittingly making a bad situation worse by implicitly sanctioning the rejection and exclusion of a sizable group of students whose only sin is unpopularity. By doing this, he is making the life of the unpopular students even more hellish.

It is becoming increasingly clear that a large number of school administrators have been tempted to go this route. They do this because, on the surface, this intervention seems sensible and harmless. Moreover, from the perspective of a bureaucrat, it is a self-serving response. Here's why: If, in the aftermath of the Columbine massacre, my grandson's principal did nothing, and a shooting subsequently took place in his school, he would be in serious trouble. But if a shooting took place after he had made an attempt to identify the "weird loners," very few people would fault him—even though it might have been his action that exacerbated the tension and, therefore, contributed to the outcome. It is for this reason that school administrators will want to do something—anything—that will keep them from looking as though they are not attempting to address the problem. In my opinion, this is a formula for disaster.

If my reasoning has merit, it might serve to underscore the importance of refusing to rush in with half-baked interventions that have not been properly researched. But we parents are understandably impatient. We crave action. If there is something dangerously broken in our schools, we want to fix it—and fix it fast. We are reluctant to wait for scientific social psychologists to get around to doing the research that will lead the way to better outcomes.

The good news is that we don't need to wait for the research. The relevant research has already been done. Indeed, scientific social psychologists have been doing careful research on these issues for years. We have discovered and tested ways of transforming the general atmosphere of schools from highly competitive, cliquish, exclusionary places—places where you would be shunned if you were from the "wrong" race or the "wrong" ethnic group, came from the wrong side of the tracks, wore the wrong kind of clothes, were too short or too fat, too tall or too thin, or just "didn't fit in"—into places where students have learned to appreciate one another and to experience empathy, compassion, and respect for one another. I have witnessed this on countless occasions: Students who had been prejudiced against each other because of racial or ethnic differences—or simply because they looked or acted differently—actually become close friends.

My colleagues and I have accomplished these minor miracles in two main ways: The first involves teaching youngsters specific ways to gain greater control over their own impulses and how to get along with others so they can resolve interpersonal conflicts amicably. This will be described in Chapter 5. The second way involves the simple device of structuring the classroom experience so that it promotes cooperation rather than competition and, in the process, motivating students to listen respectfully to one another, help one another, and begin to care about one another. They learn all this while they are in the process of learning history, geography, biology, and all the traditional academic subjects—and learning them as well or better than they would in more traditional classrooms. This approach will be described in Chapter 6.

Unlike the first strategy, the second does not require any new curricular material; it simply involves teaching traditional material in a nontraditional structure, where children pull together rather than compete against one another. My research and the research of my colleagues has demonstrated over and over again that, after working closely with one another in a cooperative way, students begin to see positive qualities in their classmates they hadn't seen before. Within a few weeks of these experiences, artificial barriers of exclusion begin to recede, and a general atmosphere of compassion, respect, and inclusion eventually prevails. Moreover, these positive outcomes are not accomplished at the expense of academics. On the contrary, in these classrooms the academic performance of most youngsters is enhanced—that is, youngsters score higher on achievement tests than they do in traditional, more competitive classrooms.

This is not a pie-in-the-sky solution. Over the past three decades, my colleagues and I have done careful scientific research on these cooperative strategies of learning and have applied them with great success in hundreds of schools all over the country. These findings just need to be implemented more broadly, so that every youngster in the country can have an opportunity to experience the benefits of being socially included. In the following chapters, we will present the relevant information and discuss the best ways to implement cooperative learning strategies, as well as other educational reforms—reforms that are important, humane, and, best of all, doable.

Wait a minute. If social psychologists have had this knowledge for more than two decades, then why wasn't it put into more general practice a long time ago? Unfortunately, a wide gulf exists between the scientific findings social psychologists uncover and the utilization of these findings by the relevant segments of our society. Most social psychologists publish the results of their experiments in rather esoteric journals that are read primarily by other social psychologists—not by the general public or policy makers. Moreover, unlike the results from medical research, most social psychological findings are not picked up by the mass media and do not find their way onto the evening news.

It's not the fault of the media; by and large, we social psychologists have not done a very good job of making our findings accessible to the average person. (As an aside, I am inclined to state that this is not always the case. Given a financial incentive, all kinds of people have been able to ferret out useful social psychological knowledge published in our obscure journals. Advertising copywriters and marketers have made use of our research on such phenomena as the power of familiarity on persuasion and the importance of scarcity in increasing the attractiveness of a product. Corporation executives have studied our research on effective leadership. People who manage political campaigns know something of our work on the relative effectiveness of positive or negative messages. Writers of books aimed at helping couples achieve marital happiness have delved into our research on the antecedents of interpersonal attraction.)

Unfortunately, it often takes a tragedy like Columbine to arouse the general public's interest in changing the atmosphere in our schools and to motivate social psychologists to make our research more accessible to people who can make use of it: parents, teachers, policy makers, and ordinary citizens. Knowledge is power. Fortified with knowledge of proven, effective classroom interventions, parents and teachers can take action to make their children's school not only a safer place, but also a more humane and more compassionate place. That is why I have written this book.

Let me restate the aim of this book as clearly and as succinctly as I can: It is my contention that those students who killed their fellow students in schools across the country were undergoing intense stress as a result of having been excluded, mocked, and taunted. There is no doubt that their behavior was both pathological and inexcusable. In my judgment, their behavior was the pathological tip of a very large iceberg. The general atmosphere of exclusion means that a great many students are having a miserable time in middle school and high school. Accordingly, the aim of this book is not simply to try to prevent pathological "losers" from killing their fellow students. It is to create a classroom atmosphere where there *are* no losers. In that very real sense, this book is about creating an atmosphere in which there is nobody left to hate. It is intended to provide parents and teachers with the tools to make schools more humane and more compassionate places, without sacrificing the basic academic material students are supposed to learn. There is nothing mutually exclusive about learning biology, literature, and calculus while also learning important human values. On the contrary, as John Dewey, America's greatest educational philosopher, indicated almost a century ago, there is every reason to believe that the one will enhance the other.

2

SOME THINGS YOU NEED TO KNOW ABOUT HUMANS AS SOCIAL ANIMALS

Before we can go deeply into the causes and potential cures of the mass killings in our nation's schools, we need to know a couple of fundamental facts about humans as social animals. One of the most important things we need to know is the enormous power a social situation can exert on individual behavior. It is a truism that humans are social animals—that we are all deeply influenced by other people and the ways they treat us, as well as by the general social climate of any situation. For example, if you are working in a fast-food restaurant where your boss is a warm and gracious woman who always treats you fairly and your coworkers are friendly, helpful, and fun to be around, chances are you would be happier, less tense, and more inclined to treat the customers kindly than if you were working for a gruff, hostile, domineering individual who was forever finding fault and your coworkers tended to snarl at you and call you derogatory names.

This is so obvious that it is hardly worth stating—if it weren't for the existence of the second fundamental fact you need to know: Ironically, although each of us is greatly influenced by the power of the social situation, we tend to underestimate the degree of influence the situation exerts on other people and to overestimate the impact of their personalities as determinants of their behavior. So whenever we observe someone's negative or nasty behavior, we are prone to assume that the behavior is caused by the kind of person they are, rather than the kind of situation they are in. Interestingly, we are almost always more generous in interpreting the reasons behind our own behavior—primarily because each of us is more familiar with the situational pressures under which we are operating. For example, if I cut you off in traffic, I know it is not something I usually do but it is because of a rare, specific situation—perhaps I am running late for my daughter's soccer game and it is important to her that I arrive on time. But if you were to cut me off in traffic, I would be apt to leap to the conclusion that you did it because you are a reckless and inconsiderate jerk.

Let me give you a more elaborate example that might clarify this important human tendency. Suppose you stop at a roadside restaurant for a cup of coffee and a piece of pie. The waitress comes over to take your order, but you are having a hard time deciding which kind of pie to order. While you are hesitating, the waitress impatiently taps her pen against her order book, rolls her eyes toward the ceiling, scowls at you, and finally snaps, "Hey, I haven't got all day, you know!"

What do you conclude about this event? When faced with such a situation, most people would conclude that the waitress is a nasty or unpleasant person; consequently, they would be reluctant to enter that particular restaurant again—especially when *that* nasty person was on duty. That would certainly be understandable.

But suppose I were to provide you with some additional information about the waitress: She is a single parent and was kept awake all night because she was nursing her youngest child, who has a painful terminal illness. On her way to work this morning, her car broke down and she is terribly worried because she has no idea where she will find the money to have it repaired. Moreover, when she finally arrived at the restaurant, she learned that her coworker was too drunk to work—requiring her to cover twice the usual number of tables—and the short-order cook keeps screaming at her because she is not picking up the orders fast enough to please him. Given all that information, you might want to revise your judgment and conclude that she is not necessarily a nasty person—just an ordinary person under enormous stress. The important fact is that in the absence of situational information almost all of us leap to the frequently erroneous conclusion that the behavior is caused entirely by flaws in the person's character or personality.

A clever experiment by social psychologist Lee Ross and his colleagues illustrates how completely we underestimate the power of the situation in explaining the behavior of other people. Ross and his colleagues set up their experiment in a "quiz show" format in which, like most quiz shows, there were two people involved: a questioner and a contestant. The questioner's job was to compose difficult questions; the contestant's job was to try to answer them. At the outset, they flipped a coin to see who would be the questioner and who would be the contestant. An observer watched the quiz show and then rated the questioner's and the contestant's general knowledge and overall intelligence. Try to put yourself in the role of the observer. What do you see? If you are not extremely careful, you will see one very smart, knowledgeable person and one rather stupid person.

But please take a closer look. Notice how the situation determines the behavior of the participants. The questioner is likely to come up with some fairly difficult questions based on some specific esoteric knowledge he just happens to possess. "In what baseball park did Babe Ruth hit his second to last home run?" "What is the capital city of Lithuania?" and "What is the date of Thomas Jefferson's death?" Simply by *asking* these questions, the questioner looks smart. On the other hand, the contestant is faced with answering these difficult questions for which he is unprepared and is likely to miss a few. This makes him look a little stupid. And this is exactly what Ross and his colleagues found. The observers judged the questioners as being far more knowledgeable and intelligent than the contestants. However, since everyone was randomly assigned to their roles, it is extremely unlikely that every single one of the questioners in the experiment was actually more knowledgeable and more intelligent than every single one of the contestants. What is most interesting is that the observers knew that the participants had been randomly assigned to these roles—they saw the coin being flipped. Yet they failed to consider the power of this situation in making their judgments about the quiz show participants. They fell into the trap of attributing what they saw to personal qualities rather than situational constraints.

What this experiment and dozens of others like it have illustrated is that when trying to account for a person's behavior in a complex situation, the overwhelming majority of people will jump to the conclusion that the behavior was caused entirely by the personality of the individual involved. And this fact—that we often fail to take the situation into account—is important to a social psychologist, for it has a profound impact on how human beings relate to one another.

NORMAL PEOPLE IN ABNORMAL SITUATIONS

Those two phenomena are important aspects of human nature: As human beings, we are deeply influenced by the social situation in which we operate, and we all underestimate the power the social situation has on the behavior of the people around us. Let me illustrate this by citing a couple of horrendous events from our recent history:

The Massacre at Jonestown. In 1978, when the Reverend Jim Jones sounded the alert, virtually all the members of the People's Temple settlement in Guyana gathered before him. Jones knew that earlier that day, under his instruction, his henchmen had murdered several people who were members of a congressional investigation team and that the sanctity and isolation of Jonestown would soon be violated. Jones proclaimed that rather than submit to this violation it was time for all of his followers to die voluntarily. Vats of poison were prepared and amidst only a few scattered shouts of protest or acts of resistance mothers and fathers administered the fatal mixture to their infants and children, drank it themselves, and lay down, arm in arm, waiting to die. More than nine hundred people died that day—either by their own hand or at the hands of their parents.

The Heaven's Gate Suicides. On March 26, 1997, thirty-nine people were found dead at a luxury estate in Rancho Santa Fe, California—participants in a mass suicide. They were all members of an obscure cult called Heaven's Gate, founded by Marshall Herff Applewhite, a former college professor. Each body was laid out neatly, feet clad in brand-new black Nikes, face covered with a purple shroud. The cult members died willingly and peacefully—and didn't really consider it suicide. They left behind detailed videotapes describing their beliefs and intentions: They believed the Hale-Bopp Comet, at the time clearly visible in the western sky, was their ticket to a new life in paradise. They were convinced that in the wake of the comet there was a gigantic spaceship whose mission was to carry them off to a new incarnation. To be picked up by the spaceship, they first needed to rid themselves of their current "containers." That is, they needed to leave their own bodies by ending their lives. Needless to say, in actuality, there was no spaceship following the comet.

Let me ask you a serious question: What were the followers of Jim Jones and Marshall Herff Applewhite like? What can you tell me about their personalities? If you are like most people, you will have a ready answer: Almost everyone we have asked is quick to conclude that there is something wrong with the personalities of these people—that they are unusually docile, unusually weak-minded, easily influenced. Perhaps they are crazy; after all, who would take their own life or kill their own children?

This may be true. There is no way to be sure. But it is hard for me to accept the fact that more than nine hundred people in the single location of Jonestown could all be extraordinarily weak, docile, or crazy—or that each and every one of the thirty-nine members of Heaven's Gate (without a single dissenter) could be unbalanced in the same way.

Rather, I rely on a rule of thumb that I sometimes call Aronson's First Law: People who do crazy things are not necessarily crazy. Sometimes, the social situation is so powerful that an overwhelming majority of ordinary, sane people—people like you or me—would behave in a strange manner.

As I said, when we are dealing with events like the Jonestown and Heaven's Gate suicides, there is no way to conclude with absolute certainty that these people were not unusual to begin with. Perhaps only weak-minded people are attracted to charismatic leaders like Jim Jones or Marshall Herff Applewhite. It is precisely for this reason that social psychologists sometimes do experiments: to try to capture the essence of a complex event under controlled scientific conditions, so that we can clarify what might be going on. In this domain, one of the most dramatic instances of Aronson's First Law stems from a classic series of experiments on obedience by Stanley Milgram. The beauty of Milgram's experiments is that he was not dealing with followers of cult leaders or with people who might be labeled as abnormally weak-minded. The participants in Milgram's experiment were a random sample of normal people like you and me.

In Milgram's experiment, people answered an advertisement to participate in a research project investigating how people learn and remember. But this was just the cover story; actually, it was a study of the extent to which people will obey authority.

Picture the scene: When the volunteer appears at the lab for his appointment, he is paired with another participant and they are approached by a somewhat stern experimenter in a white technician's coat who explains that they will be testing the effects of punishment on learning. The exercise requires one participant, the learner, to memorize a list of word pairs on which the other participant, the teacher, will test him. The volunteer and his partner draw slips to determine roles; the volunteer draws the role of teacher. He is led to a complex-looking electrical apparatus labeled Shock Generator, which has an instrument panel with a row of thirty toggle switches, calibrated from a low point of 15 volts (labeled Slight Shock) and extending through toggle switches labeled Moderate Shock and Severe Shock to a high of 450 volts (labeled xxx). By throwing the successive switches, the teacher is to deliver an increasingly intense shock each time the learner fails to answer correctly.

After receiving these instructions, the teacher follows the experimenter and the learner into the next room, where the learner is strapped into an electric chair apparatus and is attached by electrodes to the shock generator. In response to the learner's inquiry about his mild heart condition, the experimenter reassures him, "Although the shocks can be extremely painful, they cause no permanent tissue damage."

In actuality, the learner knows that he needn't worry because he is an accomplice of the experimenter. The drawing to assign roles was rigged so that he would play the role of the learner and the only real participant in the experiment is the person playing the role of the teacher. The learner is not really wired to the electricity. But the teacher firmly believes that the learner in the next room is hooked up to the shock machine that he operates. It is all very convincing. The teacher even gets a sample shock so that he is fully convinced that the shock generator is active and powerful. In the course of the experiment, he hears what he thinks is the learner reacting as if he is really being hurt. The teacher does not realize that what he is actually hearing is a tape recording, or that the learner is answering according to a prepared script. These staged events leave him absolutely convinced that the shocks are extremely painful.

As the exercise begins, the learner responds correctly several times but then begins to make mistakes. With each error, the teacher throws the next switch, supposedly administering a shock of increasing intensity. With the fifth shock, at 75 volts, the learner begins to grunt and moan. At 150 volts, he asks to be let out of the experiment. At 180 volts, he cries out that he can't stand the pain. As the shock levels approach the point labeled DANGER: EXTREME SHOCK, the teacher hears the learner pound the wall and beg to be let out of the room. But this, of course, does not constitute a correct response, so the experimenter instructs the teacher to increase the voltage and deliver the next shock by throwing the next switch.

Who were the teachers in these experiments? They were a random sample of businessmen, professional men, white-collar workers, and blue-collar workers living in and around New Haven, Connecticut. What percentage of these people continued to administer shocks to the very end of the experiment? First, let me ask you: How long would you have continued? Every year in my social psychology class, I describe

Milgram's basic procedure and I pose these questions. Every year some ninety-nine percent of the 240 students in the class indicate that they are absolutely certain they would not continue to administer shocks after the learner began to pound on the wall. The guesses made by my students are consistent with the results of Milgram's survey of forty psychiatrists at Yale Medical School. The psychiatrists predicted that most participants would quit at 150 volts, when the learner first asks to be freed. These psychiatrists also predicted that only about four percent of the participants would continue to shock the victim after he refused to respond (at 300 volts), and that less than one percent would administer the highest shock on the generator.

How do participants respond when they are actually in the situation? Milgram found, in the typical study as described above, that the great majority of his participants—more than sixty-four percent—continued to administer shocks to the very end of the experiment. The obedient participants did not continue administering shocks because they were particularly sadistic or cruel people. When Milgram compared participants' scores on a series of standardized personality tests, he discovered no differences between individuals who were fully obedient and those who successfully resisted the pressure to obey. Nor were obedient participants insensitive to the apparent plight of their victim. Some protested; many participants were observed to sweat, tremble, stutter, or show other signs of tension, and they occasionally had fits of nervous laughter. But they continued to obey to the very end of the experiment.

This behavior is not limited to American men living in Connecticut. Wherever the Milgram procedure has been tried it has produced a similar degree of obedience. For example, several replications of the experiment have demonstrated that people in Australia, Jordan, Spain, Germany, and Holland react in much the same way Milgram's participants did. Similarly, women have been found to be at least as obedient as men.

Again, I want to emphasize the fact that the people in these experiments had no idea that the victim of their obedience was not really hooked up to the shock apparatus. They firmly believed that they were doing great harm to the individual. And yet, almost two out of every three people obeyed to the very end. Whenever I describe the experiment to groups of people, their first impulse is to suggest that the people who delivered these shocks must be crazy. Their behavior is certainly bizarre. But are they crazy? I don't think so. The word *crazy* loses all meaning if it applies to sixty-four percent of the population.

What this experiment illustrates beautifully is the immense power of the social situation. And what is illustrated by the behavior of the people to whom I describe the experiment is a strong tendency to underestimate just how powerful the social situation can be; their initial inclination is to consider those obedient participants crazy. As I said earlier, most of us have a tendency to explain unpleasant behavior by attaching a label to the perpetrator ("crazy," "sadistic," or whatever), thereby excluding that person from the rest of "us nice people." In that way, we need not worry about the unpleasant behavior, because it has nothing to do with us nice folks. Several months after the Columbine massacre, Joanne Jacobs, one of my favorite editorial writers, asserted that Harris and Klebold committed those murders not out of rage or revenge, but simply because they were evil. I appreciate her reasoning, but where does it lead us? Based on her analysis, what can we do to prevent future shootings? Detect evil in youngsters before they act and remove them from society? I don't think that would be possible or desirable.

This kind of analysis is problematic for at least two reasons. First, it tends to make us smug about our own susceptibility to negative situational pressures. If we believe that any distasteful action can be committed only by evil people, then it follows that there is no way that my friends or I could ever be provoked into doing anything so wrongheaded. Let's return for a moment to the participants in Stanley Milgram's experiment on obedience. Were the obedient teachers in Milgram's experiment evil? Perhaps they were. They certainly perpetrated an atrocious act—delivering apparently lethal shocks in blind obedience to an authority figure. But please note that these people constitute sixty-four percent of the normal population. Are my friends and I incapable of such obedient behavior? Perhaps. But I wouldn't bet on it.

Second, this kind of analysis serves as a smoke screen that diverts our attention away from trying to gain an understanding of the complexities of human behavior. By looking for answers *only* in terms of the weakness or evil of the particular wrongdoers, we are prone to neglect to examine relevant elements of the situation. But it is of paramount importance that we attempt to understand how different social situations can lead to different outcomes. Only then can we hope to come up with sensible solutions to complex societal problems.

COULD ANYONE HAVE PREDICTED THE COLUMBINE MASSACRE?

In the beginning of the chapter I gave you two basic facts about humans as social animals as a way of inviting you to take another look at the behavior of Eric Harris and Dylan Klebold, the shooters in the Columbine massacre. I have described their behavior as pathological—and I want to repeat that here. Ordinary human beings do not bring weapons to school and kill their classmates. The question is: Was their behavior caused by a deep-seated inner pathology ("craziness" or "evil")? Had they been crazy or evil for a number of years and people around them just hadn't noticed? Or was there something about the situation they were in that triggered the pathological behavior? We will probably never answer that question definitively. But understanding the power of the situation they were in might help us find ways to reduce future outbreaks of this lethal violence.

Let's take a quick look at Eric Harris. At Columbine, he was generally considered to be an awkward outsider, somewhat creepy, not a regular guy. Was he a misfit? Well, yes.

Was he *always* a misfit? I don't think so. The description of Eric as a "creepy" person would have astonished Eric's class-mates in Plattsburgh, New York, where he lived before his family moved to Littleton. In Plattsburgh, he was well-liked, played Little League baseball, and hung out with a popular group. This doesn't sound like the same person. I think it's important to realize that he *is* the same person—someone who found himself in a new and different social situation and experienced a great deal of difficulty being accepted by his new peer group. Needless to say, this is certainly not intended as a justification for his behavior. Typically, when teenagers move to a new town they have difficulty adjusting to their new situation, partly because the social climate in most high schools is not very welcoming. They suffer, but they usually do not act out in a drastic manner. I bring it up not as a justification, but in an attempt to gain some under-standing—as a way of underscoring everything I have been saying about the enormous impact a change in the social sit-uation can have on the way we are regarded, the way we behave, and how we come to feel about ourselves.

A deeply touching case in point is Cassie Bernall, one of the students who was killed at Columbine. It was widely reported that just prior to being shot she professed her firm belief in God.* Inspired by her last words, her parents wrote

---

*In point of fact, there is some controversy about this incident. Some eyewitnesses have attributed this statement to a different student.

a book about their life with Cassie as a teenager. Although she was a loving daughter at the time of her death, this was not always the case. A few years earlier, she seemed a lot like Harris and Klebold. She was rebellious, nihilistic, dabbled in the occult, and secretly practiced witchcraft. Moreover, her parents report that they found letters in her room expressing hatred of them and threatening to kill them. Horrified, her parents showed the letters to the police. The police informed them that these were some of the most vile, monstrous letters they had ever seen. What did the parents do? They initiated a radical change in Cassie's situation, pulling her out of her public school and sending her to a Christian school. At first, she was sullen and defiant, but gradually the layers of hardness and anger began to peel away as she became increasingly receptive to this more wholesome environment provided by the Christian school. After a time, her parents became convinced that the real Cassie had come back to them again and they developed enough confidence in her to let her attend a public school again. At the time of her death, they were delighted with the adjustment she had made.

Who was the real Cassie? The loving youngster who, at the time of her death, was filled with a strong religious faith or the angry youngster filled with hatred and murderous thoughts toward her parents? To Cassie Bernall—who, like all teenagers, was in the process of developing a moral compass—the immediate social environment played a vital role in determining the path she eventually took. Could the same be said of Eric Harris and Dylan Klebold? The possibility is certainly worth a closer look.

Given that the behavior of Harris and Klebold was pathological, is it reasonable to ask whether it could have been predicted—like a hurricane or a flood? The Centers for Disease Control and Prevention maintains a department that is devoted to the study of violence. The scientists working in this department have become pretty good at predicting out-breaks of violence in our nation's hot spots as a function of specific events—like the riots and looting that took place in South Central Los Angeles immediately following the initial acquittal of the police officers who beat up Rodney King. But these scientists are among the first to admit that they could not have predicted the massacre at Columbine High School—or any of the other multiple school shootings in the recent past. Moreover, these scientists suggest that, in situa-tions like this, it is most often the case that no matter how plugged in the parents or how vigilant the teachers, there is no way that they could have grasped the intentions of the perpetrators in advance of the act.

Let me be clear: I am not asserting that close scrutiny of the shooters Eric Harris and Dylan Klebold—including a search of their bedrooms—would not have tipped us off. What I am suggesting is that there was very little about their day-to-day public behavior that would have led us to conclude that they were dangerous individuals. They were functioning well in school, doing their homework, prepar-ing for exams, getting reasonably good grades, and so on.

They weren't popular with their fellow students, but they weren't exacly loners either; they did have a few friends. Indeed, on the weekend prior to the massacre, Klebold had a date for the high school prom and, along with Harris (who didn't have a date), attended some of the post-prom social events, partying with some of the very students whose lives they were about to put in jeopardy.

This is not to imply that Harris and Klebold were your average, trouble-free, typical American boys either. They were not. In terms of academic performance, they were actually above average. But they certainly had their problems. For one thing, it is clear that they did not get along well with most of their classmates—especially the school athletes and other students in the "in-group." Their classmates thought of them as outsiders. They were labeled "goths" because they dressed in black, wore trenchcoats in all kinds of weather, and kept pretty much to themselves. Their classmates frequently taunted them with epithets like "faggot," although there is no indication that they were homosexual. They also enjoyed playing violent video games. Moreover, they had recently been in trouble with the law, having been apprehended and punished for breaking into a car and stealing electronic equipment. One of them (Eric Harris) was under psychiatric care at the time of the massacre and was taking antidepressant medication.

Do these characteristics mark them as crazy or as potential killers? I don't think so. If we tried to protect our schools from every student who wasn't particularly popular, who dressed strangely, or who enjoyed violent video games, then we would be guarding our schools against most of the student body. If we were to regard everyone who is in therapy for mild depression as a potential threat to our safety, then we would be creating a nightmarish situation for them—as well as for us. *Time* magazine recently reported that in a typical high school about twenty percent of the students are taking medication for depression and other psychiatric disorders. Think about it. Do we really want to further isolate the hundreds of thousands of students who are being treated for depression—depression that may have been induced (at least in part) by isolation in the first place? I don't think so. Moreover, some of the things that distinguish Harris and Klebold from most of their classmates lend credence to the notion that their murderous rampage could not have been easily predicted. True, Eric Harris was seeing a psychiatrist regularly, but the psychiatrist, a competent professional, was startled and flabbergasted by the news of the shootings. Here was a highly trained therapist, an expert on human behavior and pathology, who apparently had access to some of Eric's innermost thoughts, and yet he did not consider the young man to be prone to overt violence.

In addition, following the burglary, the court officer who supervised Harris and Klebold in the juvenile rehabilitation program recommended by the court was enthusiastic about their future. Less than three months before the massacre, he described Harris this way: "Eric is a very bright young man who is likely to succeed in life. He is intelligent enough to achieve lofty goals as long as he stays on task and remains motivated." Of Klebold, the officer said: "He is intelligent enough to make any dream a reality but he needs to understand hard work is part of it."

What about their family life? Did Harris and Klebold come from broken homes? Were their parents uncaring, alcoholic, neglectful, or abusive? No—on all counts. Both boys came from stable, comfortable, middle-class, two-parent families. As far as we can judge, the Harrises and the Klebolds were model citizens and, from all appearances, they were better than average parents. There was nothing on the surface to lead to a prediction of violence. One of the most striking facts brought to light by the videotapes made by Harris and Klebold a few weeks prior to the massacre was that these kids loved their parents and were concerned about them. Indeed, the only shred of remorse or regret indicated on the videos was not about the victims of the carnage they were about to commit, but about the impact their actions were bound to have on the lives of their parents. "They're going to be put through hell once we do this," Harris said. Then, addressing his parents directly, he said, "There's nothing you guys could do about this." Klebold told his mother and father that they had been great parents and went out of his way to exonerate them—as did Harris, who quoted from Shakespeare's *The Tempest* in the process: "Good wombs hath borne bad sons."

Don't get me wrong. I am not suggesting that close scrutiny of the behavior of Harris and Klebold in the months prior to the massacre would not have turned up evidence of their violent intent. There were plenty of clues as to their intentions, but these were not obvious to the casual observer—to their teachers, classmates, therapist, parole officer, neighbors, and so on. But shouldn't their parents have known? Well, yes and no. If their parents had conducted periodic searches of their bedrooms, they would have found weapons and paraphernalia for making bombs. So should all parents search the rooms of their teenagers on a regular basis? It's not a simple question. Being the parent of a teenager is a complex undertaking. After a tragic event like Columbine, it is easy for people to answer that question with a strong yes. It is easy for most parents to claim, after the fact, that that's precisely what they would have done. People use hindsight as a way of convincing themselves (incorrectly) that they would have acted in a manner consistent with their new information. But my guess is that prior to Columbine, most American parents held an attitude similar to the one I held when my kids were in their teens: I wanted to make sure my kids weren't getting themselves into trouble, but I also wanted to afford them a degree of privacy. Teenagers may have things in their bedrooms that are perfectly innocent but that might cause them embarrassment if their parents were to discover them (romantic notes, indications of masturbation, weird entries in their diary, and so on). Accordingly, unless I had reason to suspect that my teenagers were up to something dangerous (like drug use), I would not search their rooms. We will probably never know whether the Harrises or the Klebolds had reason to suspect that their kids might have been up to something.

But there was one additional clue: One might suppose that if the authorities had closely monitored Eric Harris's bizarre rantings on the Internet, they would have become suspicious. After the fact, it is easy to blame the parents for not being more vigilant, for not searching their children's rooms. After the fact, the Internet ravings seem like a clear giveaway. But prior to the actual killings, they might have easily been interpreted as the boastful words of an unhappy teenager. As a matter of fact, it turns out that the police *had* been informed about the violent things that Harris had been writing on the Internet, but had chosen not to act on them—apparently dismissing them (as you or I might have done) as idle braggadocio.

Again, it is important to understand that the situation since the Columbine massacre is very different from what it was prior to the massacre. At this point, highly sensitized by this tragic event, parents have become more vigilant (at least temporarily) and schools have adopted a zero-tolerance strategy. Thus, in the past several months students who have issued idle threats—teenagers making threats that would have been ignored or laughed off prior to April 1999—are now being expelled from school, arrested, and occasionally indicted. Schools now have very little choice but to take every threat seriously—but at a great cost in terms of the general atmosphere of the school.

Likewise, if someone had had complete access to Eric Harris's private writings, that observer might have been alerted to possible trouble, for Harris kept a diary in which he discussed, in some detail, his plan to destroy the school. Similarly, if someone had conducted a thorough search of their bedrooms, that person probably would have discovered the videotapes detailing their plans.

I want to emphasize my major point here: There were clues to their intent (squirreled away in their bedrooms and displayed on the Internet), but the day-to-day aspects of Harris's and Klebold's lives did not manifest behavior that would lead their parents, teachers, school officials, or psychiatrist to predict their shooting spree.

This situation is far from unique. It is typically the case when a rather ordinary person suddenly picks up a gun and starts shooting. After the fact, there is usually someone who will tell you that his behavior had been a little strange lately. After the fact, the "warning signs" always glow brighter and seem more obvious than they did beforehand. After the fact, there will always be people who will feel guilty for not having noticed these warning signs or who will blame those who they feel should have noticed them. After the fact, there will be a short period of time when all loners who dress strangely will come under close scrutiny and when parents, teachers, and school administrators will scrutinize the Internet and other media. After the fact, there will always be those who will want to arrest and incarcerate any unhappy youngster who makes an idle threat. This is understandable. But, blessedly, this increased surveillance will not last long. There are simply too many harmless, meaningless warning signs out there. The fact of the matter is that these well-meaning scrutinizers are looking in the wrong place.

As troubling as it might seem, none of us are particularly good at predicting such behavior. This lack of predictability usually comes as a surprise to most people—accustomed as we are to the genre of the mystery novel or film in which there is a clear villain, where once the villain is exposed, the problem is solved. Real life is seldom so simple. But the fact that the massacre probably could not have been predicted doesn't mean that it could not have been prevented. For prevention, we must not confine ourselves to an analysis of the minds of the shooters. We must take a look at the broader social environment in which the two shooters were embedded.

3

DEALING WITH DISASTERS, PART 1

Pump-Handle Interventions

There are a great many dangers and disasters out there: lethal diseases, traffic fatalities, earthquakes, hurricanes, violent crimes, hate crimes, drug addiction, alcohol addiction, and the like. And our society has developed a great many strategies for dealing with them. Basically, these strategies fit into two broad categories. One of these attempts to get directly at the basic cause of the problem. I call these "root cause interventions." The other deals with more peripheral aspects of the problem. I call these "pump-handle interventions." In this chapter, I will deal with the more peripheral, pump-handle interventions to school violence.

Let me give you the defining example of a peripheral, pump-handle intervention. It took place during the 1854 cholera epidemic in London. Dr. John Snow, a legendary British physician, attempted to find out what, if anything, the people stricken with cholera might have had in common and how they might differ from those not stricken. Through some pretty careful detective work, Dr. Snow managed to trace the epidemic to a particular well where he surmised that the water was contaminated. Initially, he made no attempt to find the reason for the contamination or how it got there. He made no attempt to clean up the water. He did not even try to educate the people living in the area or to try to persuade them to refrain from drinking water from that well. He simply removed the pump handle from the wellhead. This simple action completely stanched the epidemic.

GUNS, GUNS, GUNS!

Just as Dr. Snow noted that cholera seemed to be coming from a single well, we can look for common factors underlying multiple killings in schools. Considering the most recent incidents—those that took place in the past two or three years—there is one factor that leaps out at us: The perpetrators all used guns to which they had easy access. This is not surprising to any American. In our country guns are ubiquitous and play an important role in the lives of many of our citizens—and, unfortunately, are a major cause of the violent deaths of many of our citizens. Tragically, teenagers seem to be able to get their hands on guns without much trouble. This is particularly true of teenagers living in rural and suburban areas: According to a recent poll, sixty-three percent of rural and suburban teenagers admitted to either owning a gun or living in a household where they had easy access to a gun; this was the case for thirty-two percent of urban teenagers.

The National Rifle Association (NRA) is fond of its slogan—"Guns don't kill people, people do." In a sense, they are right. But make no mistake about it, the presence of guns in a home increases the probability that young people will use them on other young people. For a quick and vivid comparison, let's look at a pair of cities separated by the Canadian border: Seattle, Washington, and Vancouver, British Columbia. They are twin cities in a lot of ways: They have similar climates, populations, and economies. They also have almost identical general crime rates and rates of physical assault. People who live in Seattle are not prone to be more violent than people who live across the border in Vancouver. But there is one major difference: Aggression in Seattle is far more likely to be lethal than aggression in Vancouver; the murder rate in Seattle is more than twice as high as that in Vancouver. This is almost certainly due to the fact that Vancouver severely restricts gun ownership, while Seattle does not. It is simply easier to kill one or more people with a gun than with a knife, a baseball bat, or one's fists.

Sociologist Dane Archer and his colleagues have examined violence in countries from all parts of the world, and they find that the homicide rate is highly correlated with the availability of guns. For example, Britain, where handguns are banned, has one-fourth the population of the United States and one-sixteenth the number of annual homicides. Following up on these data, Archer asked teenagers from the United States and ten other countries to read incomplete stories involving conflict among people and to supply their own guess as to the outcome of the conflict. American teenagers were far more likely to anticipate a violent conclusion to the conflict than teenagers from any other country. Moreover, the violent conclusions drawn by American teenagers were far more likely to be lethal, gunladen, and merciless than those by teenagers in any of the other countries. The conclusion is undeniable: Lethal violence, especially with guns, is a major part of American society. This is why it plays such a major role in the expectations and fantasies of young Americans.

There is a sense in which the National Rifle Association is correct: Guns are not the root cause of the recent school killings. But it would be naive to suggest that their easy availability did not play a major role in these tragic events. Can we apply some version of the pump-handle intervention to the issue of school killings?

Yes and no. On the surface, the simplest, most direct, and most complete version of the pump-handle intervention would be to eliminate all guns from our society: No pump handle: a sharp reduction in the drinking of tainted water; no guns: a sharp reduction in multiple killings in our schools—and everywhere else, for that matter. Needless to say, this would be impossible. We would have to confiscate every gun in America. But in America, we believe in individual liberties, so it should not surprise you that an overwhelming majority of the population opposes the confiscation of guns.

A less extreme and far more feasible application of the pump-handle intervention would require the licensing of guns and restricting juveniles' access to guns. This would not be a complete solution, but it certainly would be a giant step in the direction of greater school safety. Specifically, to achieve this goal Congress would need to pass legislation requiring gun owners (like automobile drivers) to be licensed, requiring gun owners to use gun locks or so-called "smart" guns, and forbidding the sale of guns to minors in stores, at gun shows, by individuals—and strictly enforcing that restriction. Unfortunately, given the current political climate, even such limited legislation appears to be highly unlikely. Following the assassination of a leader such as John F. Kennedy or Martin Luther King, Jr., or a major killing of innocents like the Columbine massacre, there is usually an increased call for additional gun control legislation. But after a flurry of activity, Congress invariably backs away and the proposed legislation is either bottled up or goes down in defeat.

This state of affairs is astonishing to my European and Asian friends, who live in countries where the use of guns is strictly controlled. It is particularly astonishing considering the fact, according to a Gallup poll taken in May of 1999, that the overwhelming majority of Americans see the easy availability of guns as being among our most serious national problems and would support laws forbidding the sale of guns to minors. As a matter of fact, according to this poll, even the majority of gun owners now favor legislation making guns less dangerous and less available to the violent, the deranged, and the young.

It seems, once again, that the vast majority of the American people—being opposed to the confiscation of guns but in favor of gun control laws—probably have the right idea. Let's take a closer look. Extremists on both sides of the gun issue are adamant in their beliefs. At one extreme, the NRA argues that virtually any law restricting gun use would be unconstitutional—violating the Second Amendment's provision that it is every citizen's right to bear arms. The NRA fights every attempt to regulate the use of guns, arguing that even banning military assault weapons or requiring gun locks would be a slippery slope that would inevitably lead to further restrictions. At the other extreme, some gun control advocates argue that the framers of the Constitution did not extend the right to bear arms to all citizens, but only to "a well-regulated Militia," as the preamble to the Second Amendment specifies. Regarding constitutionality, it is interesting and important to note that most serious legal scholars come down on the side of the overwhelming majority of the American people—asserting that an outright ban of all guns would be unconstitutional; legally, the Second Amendment's clear statement regarding the people's right cannot be trumped by the preamble's statement about a well-regulated militia. At the same time, these scholars note that almost no right is absolute or unlimited—including the right to bear arms or even the right of free speech. Thus, sensible restrictions on guns are both constitutional and essential.

Given the clear public mandate favoring sensible restrictions on the availability of guns, why is Congress reluctant to pass even the simplest and least invasive of gun control laws? According to some of our most astute political observers, most legislators are not acting according to their own reasoned assessment of the issue—but are caving in to craven political expediency. Tragically, what seems to motivate most members of Congress is not the rash of recent school shootings but the fear of losing the next election. The NRA has enormous financial resources and has been known to pump millions of dollars into the campaign coffers of anyone running against a congressman targeted as a proponent of gun control legislation. As a consequence, it seems as though this particular pump-handle intervention will not be available to us—at least not in the near future.

As if to underscore this analysis, in July of 1999, while Congress was debating gun control, a group of ninety-five high school students from the Denver area—several from Littleton—flew to Washington in a vain attempt to influence the vote. Although many spoke movingly about the funerals of friends—victims of shootings—they had attended recently, their stories had little impact on members of Congress. After the vote, they confronted their own congressman, Scott McInnis of Colorado, and asked him why he had voted against a measure aimed at simply requiring background checks of people purchasing guns at gun shows. After complimenting the students on their enthusiasm, he replied by stating that lawmakers needed to make sure that they did not deprive law-abiding citizens of guns. "I have the right to protect myself," he said.

Later, three of the students talked to reporters about how it felt to have guns pointed at them. One of them, Rosa Chavez, said that the memory of that experience filled her with anger at lawmakers' inaction. "It's one thing for them to say they sympathize with our pain," she said. "It's quite another thing to look down a gun barrel and think maybe you're going to die."

METAL DETECTORS AND SECURITY GUARDS

A different form of the pump-handle intervention involves installing metal detectors and hiring security guards to monitor them at the entrance to each and every one of our schools. When I ran that idea past a group of high school students recently, their response was predictable and can be easily summarized in three words: "What a drag!"

But perhaps they can get used to it. After all, there was a time, not so long ago, when there were no metal detectors or X-ray machines at airports. I remember, some twenty-five years ago, freely walking to arrival and departure gates, pockets bulging, carrying bulky packages containing God knows what, without passing through any kind of apparatus and without being frisked. I can even remember wandering out on the tarmac, undeterred, to greet friends arriving on planes. The sudden and ominous rise of international terrorism put an end to that. Twenty-five years ago, who would have believed that metal detectors and X-ray machines would become such a ubiquitous, fully accepted part of our lives? But most travelers now take them in stride. Indeed, given the degree of destruction and loss of life that could be brought on by one political zealot or deranged individual boarding a plane with a gun or an explosive device, most of us are grateful for this minor inconvenience. At airports, metal detectors constitute an excellent pump-handle solution to the problem of guns or explosives being carried onto planes. We don't need to analyze the political gripes of terrorists or the cause of a deranged person's insanity. All we need is a good metal detector and we air travelers are relatively safe.

Hey, if metal detectors have become universally accepted in our airports and are so very effective in protecting passengers and aircraft, why not install them in all of our schools? Wouldn't that be a simple solution? Get ready now, I am about to pronounce a couple of profound truths: 1. Schools are not airports; 2. Not all schools are the same.

Airports are, by nature, impersonal places. We don't expect an airport to be a place to enjoy or in which to spend a good part of our lives—but merely as a place to pass through, a necessary transit point on our way somewhere else. We passengers realize that the aircraft we are about to board will be carrying more than two hundred strangers from several different countries with all kinds of possible agendas. When we read about a plane being hijacked or blown out of the sky, it reminds us, with a shiver, of how vulnerable we all are at 30,000 feet to the fanatical behavior of a political zealot or to the irrational actions of a disturbed individual with a gun who suddenly might decide, in midair, that he would rather go to Paris than Detroit. In that context, most of us are only too happy to go through the minor inconvenience of a metal detector as a way of protecting our lives.

Schools are very different. As youngsters, we all spent almost half of each day's waking hours in and around schools. We each have expectations about what a school should be like. Educators Ted and Nancy Sizer suggest that everything the adult community does or does not do in a school sends a message to the students—and they are quick to pick up on the message. For example, if the school building is cold and drafty, has broken windows, unswept floors, grimy walls, cracked linoleum, and leaky toilets, the students get the message that the adult community does not care a lot about their education and that any teachers working there cannot be very good or else they wouldn't be working in such a rat hole.

Schools and neighborhoods differ. The meaning of a metal detector in schools is certain to take on different meanings depending upon the context. Context is of paramount importance in determining meaning. For example, when interviewed, several teenagers living in high crime areas admitted to bringing guns into school—claiming they were doing it for self-protection. This is unfortunate; but, in the context of a high crime area, this might not be an irrational thing to do. If you are a youngster living in a high crime area, and some of your fellow students who don't like you very much are armed, it would certainly be tempting to consider carrying a gun to school yourself. In this context, when metal detectors were installed in some of these schools they had a positive effect on a great many students because it now made it both impossible and unnecessary to carry a gun into school. Most teenagers living in high crime areas stated that metal detectors made their school the safest place in the neighborhood. Indeed, in the immediate aftermath of the Columbine massacre, when schools were shut down across the country, students living in the high crime neighborhoods of some of our largest cities were incredulous because they knew that only in their school could they feel relatively safe. These observations receive firm support from a CBS/*NY Times* survey in October 1999, indicating that urban teenagers feel just as safe in school as rural teenagers.

So what's wrong with installing metal detectors in every school in the country? Again, the context is paramount. An action that might have a positive impact in some neighborhoods might have a negative effect in others. Putting metal detectors in neighborhood schools where violence is prevalent and potentially lethal makes the school a safe haven. My guess is that putting metal detectors in schools in safe, affluent neighborhoods might create the feeling that the schools are potentially dangerous. Moreover, installing metal detectors in all our schools would be tantamount to admitting that, from coast to coast, in small towns and large cities, in this, the most powerful democracy in the history of civilization, our teenagers are so dangerous and so out-of-control that we need to apply extreme measures to protect them from one another.

Finally, it should be noted that installing metal detectors would not make the schools perfectly safe. If teenagers with grievances and guns are motivated to shoot their fellow students, they can easily accomplish their mission without even entering the school building. For example, in Jonesboro, Arkansas, the shooters fired on their classmates from behind trees surrounding the school after luring their victims out of the school building by setting off the school's fire alarm.

VIOLENCE IN THE MEDIA

Does Watching Violence in the Media Make Us More Violent?

Another factor that links the shooters in each of the recent school massacres is that they all watched a lot of TV and were avid players of video games. For a great many years, developmental psychologists have been studying the effect of TV on the socialization of children and adolescents. There is no doubt that youngsters learn a great deal from watching TV. There is also no doubt that TV remains steeped in violence. According to a recent study, fifty-eight percent of all TV programs contain violence—and, of those, seventy-eight percent were without remorse, criticism, or penalty for that violence. Indeed, some forty percent of the violent incidents seen on TV were initiated by characters portrayed as heroes or other attractive role models for children. At a recent congressional hearing on TV violence, it was estimated that the average American boy has witnessed more than 100,000 acts of violence on television by the time he enters the seventh grade.

Exactly what do children learn from watching violence on TV? Almost half a century ago, psychologist Albert Bandura and his colleagues began a series of classic experiments to determine whether young children can learn aggressive behavior by observing adult models. The basic procedure in these studies was to let a child watch an adult knock around a plastic, air-filled Bobo doll (the kind that bounces back after it has been knocked down). Sometimes, the adult would accompany her physical aggression with verbal abuse against the doll. A short time later, the kids were allowed to play with the doll. In these experiments, not only did the children imitate the aggressive models, they also engaged in other, more creative forms of aggression. The children did more than simply copy the behavior of an adult. Seeing aggressive behavior served as an impetus for them to engage in more innovative aggressive behavior of their own. Why are these experiments considered so important? Who cares what happens to a Bobo doll, anyway? Let's take a closer look.

Many studies have tried to determine whether watching adults behave violently on TV has an impact on young children's aggressiveness that is still manifest in their teens. In a typical study of this kind: 1. Teenagers are asked to recall which shows they watched on TV when they were kids and how frequently they watched them; 2. The shows are independently rated in terms of their degree of violence; 3. The general aggressiveness of the teenagers is independently rated by their teachers and classmates. The major finding: The more violence youngsters watched as children, the more aggressive they were as teenagers.

But one has to be very careful in evaluating research of this kind. These results appear convincing on the surface, but network executives quickly point out that they do not *prove* that watching a lot of violence on TV actually *causes* children to become violent teenagers. Of course, network executives aren't exactly unbiased on this issue. Nevertheless, I must admit that they have a good point. As a scientist I know that simply because two factors are related, it does not necessarily mean that one causes the other. In science, we have a slogan to remind us to be cautious on that score: Correlation does not equal causality. After all, it is certainly possible that the aggressive kids were either born with a tendency to enjoy violence or they learned to enjoy it early on from their parents or from the neighborhood kids. Because they have a tendency to enjoy violence, they will also enjoy watching it on TV and they will commit more acts of violence than the average child. So it might not be the case that watching TV violence actually *causes* violent behavior; watching violence on TV may just be one of the many by-products of a proclivity toward violence.

In order to find out whether watching violence on TV actually causes aggression, we must conduct a well-controlled experiment. We won't rely on what people remember about their TV watching habits and we won't rely on mere correlations. We will take a group of young people and, by the flip of a coin, expose half of them to violent TV shows and the other half to nonviolent TV shows. We will then measure the effect of these experiences on their aggressive behavior immediately afterward. Because we assign them to the two conditions randomly, we can be quite certain that one group was not significantly more violent than the other group before the experiment started. Thus, we can conclude with a high degree of confidence that a major difference in aggressive behavior immediately after the TV experience was due to the type of show they were watching.

Social psychologists have performed this experiment a great many times. The overwhelming thrust of the experimental evidence shows that watching violence does indeed increase the frequency of aggressive behavior in children. Let me give you an example. In this experiment, the researchers had a group of children watch an extremely violent TV episode of a popular police series. In the control condition, a similar group of children were exposed to an exciting but nonviolent TV sporting event for the same length of time. Each child was then allowed to play in another room with a group of children who had not been watching anything on TV that day. Those who had watched the violent police drama showed far more aggression against their playmates than those who had watched the sporting event.

As you might expect, watching TV violence does not affect all youngsters in exactly the same manner. If a child happens to be feeling angry, frustrated, or upset at the moment, watching TV violence can push him over the edge and is more likely to produce a violent response than if he is feeling happy and relaxed. Similarly, watching violence on TV also has the greatest effect on youngsters who are chronically frustrated or unhappy or who are somewhat prone to be aggressive to begin with. Suppose you were to ask teachers to rate the aggressiveness of each of the students in their classes, then show half the students a violent film, while the other half watches a sporting event. Suppose you then turn them all loose in a game of floor hockey. What happens? The results of this experiment are clear: Watching the violent film increased the number of aggressive acts committed during the hockey game—primarily by those students who had previously been rated as highly aggressive by their teachers. These youngsters hit others with their sticks, threw elbows, and yelled hostile insults at their opponents to a much greater extent than either the youngsters rated as nonaggressive who had also watched the violent film or those rated as aggressive who had watched the nonviolent film. It is almost as if watching media violence serves to give aggressive kids permission to express their existing aggressive tendencies.

In a similar fashion, recent research shows that youngsters who spend a lot of time playing violent video games also show the greatest degree of aggression when turned loose with other youngsters after playing the video game.

The Numbing Effect of TV Violence

If we watch a lot of TV violence, does that cause us to take violence less seriously? There is a great deal of research showing that repeated exposure to painful or unpleasant events tends to have a numbing effect on our sensitivity to those events. In one experiment, the researchers measured the physiological responses of several young men while they were watching a rather brutal and bloody boxing match. Those who had watched a lot of TV in their daily lives seemed relatively indifferent to the mayhem taking place in the ring—that is, they showed little physiological evidence of excitement, anxiety, or the like. They treated the violence in a lackadaisical manner. On the other hand, those who typically watched relatively little TV underwent major physiological arousal. The violence really got to them.

What Are We to Conclude From All This Research?

The research results are clear: In spite of the protestations of media executives, exposure to violence in films, on TV, and in video games can and does have an important impact on the behavior and feelings of children and adolescents. But again, it is important that we don't get carried away. It would be erroneous to conclude that watching violence on TV was the *cause* of the kind of lethal violent behavior that took place at Columbine High School. Millions of kids watch a lot of violent stuff on TV and don't go around shooting their classmates. At the same time, it would be naive to believe that TV violence is not a contributing factor—especially if the youngsters watching all that TV are frustrated, angry, or prone to violence.

So how might one apply the pump-handle intervention? Legislatively, this is a tricky business. Congress is understandably reluctant to pass laws restricting the First Amendment rights of broadcasters, filmmakers, and the designers of video games. Moreover, even if such legislation were passed, the courts would be almost certain to find it unconstitutional. In this instance, I find myself in agreement with Congress and the courts. I would not be happy living in a country where the government dictated the kinds of entertainment we could and couldn't watch. What Congress can do is exert pressure on the entertainment industries to show some restraint, police themselves, and establish a useful rating system so that parents can attempt to exercise sensible vigilance over what their children watch. If broadcasters and filmmakers would succumb to this pressure, this would be a small step in the right direction.

SUMMARY OF PUMP-HANDLE
INTERVENTIONS

All of these pump-handle interventions have some merit. If guns were less easily available to youngsters, then it would certainly reduce the frequency of mass killings in the schools. If metal detectors were installed in all our schools and security guards roamed the corridors and schoolyards, then there would certainly be fewer killings in and around our schools (though this would come at a heavy psychological price). If we could find a reasonable way to encourage producers of films, TV dramas, and video games to drastically reduce the violence, then I am certain it would have a salutary effect on the behavior of our youngsters. There is no reason that each of these peripheral interventions cannot be applied with sense and sensitivity. To induce Congress to pass reasonable gun control laws, extremists on both sides of the issue must step back a bit. Extremists on one end of the continuum must accept the fact that we are never going to get rid of all guns; extremists on the other end of the continuum must accept the fact that we must pass laws to require locks on guns and to keep guns out of the hands of children. Metal detectors and increased security can be useful in some communities—but in other communities they may cause more harm than good. The decision must be made in a rational manner by each community after a careful assessment of its own risks and needs. Finally, given that government censorship of the media would be obnoxious, it would be of great benefit to society if the media would monitor itself and decide to peddle a good deal less of that stuff to our youngsters.

As useful as pump-handle interventions may be, they fall short in the final analysis. They are not addressing the central problem. For millions of youngsters, middle school and high school are stressful places—and much of that stress is unnecessary. There are only a small number of students who respond to that stress by lethally lashing out at their fellow students, but the number of students who are unhappy, anxious, and depressed—to the point of contemplating suicide—is much larger than most parents realize.

THE SHOOTERS WERE ADOLESCENT BOYS

Before leaving this chapter, I should point out that there is at least one additional element that all the school massacres had in common: All of the shooters were adolescent boys—obviously. I say "obviously" because 1. The shootings took place in or around middle schools and high schools—places that are populated by adolescents; and 2. Girls, although fully capable of verbal aggression, physical violence, and even murder, have almost never committed mass murder. So what is there about being an adolescent boy?

As everyone knows, adolescence is a time of physical growth and sexual maturation—a time of incredibly huge and rapid physiological and hormonal changes. But these changes follow rather different paths for boys and for girls.

Adolescent girls experience a sharp increase in the production of estrogen, develop breasts and pubic hair, and begin menstruating. Adolescent boys are flooded with testosterone, begin to grow facial hair and pubic hair, undergo a changing voice, witness significant growth in their testes and penis, and experience ejaculation. When I say that adolescent boys are "flooded" with testosterone, I am not exaggerating: Adolescent boys have testosterone levels up to eighteen times as great as childhood levels. (For girls the comparable difference in estrogen levels between childhood and adolescence is much smaller.) Testosterone is a hormone that is not only associated with sex; it is also associated with aggression. As one indication of this association, it has been shown that convicts serving time in penitentiaries for violent crimes have considerably higher testosterone levels than those serving time for nonviolent crimes.

For both boys and girls, being accepted by their peer group becomes increasingly important—even vital—during adolescence. It is out of a strong desire to be included that youngsters are tempted to dress alike, follow the crowd to the tattoo parlor and the body piercer, develop similar taste in music, films, foods, and so on. It always hurts to be rejected. But, at this particular stage of our development, rejection can be excruciatingly painful. Although it is tempting for us parents to dismiss our teenagers' machinations as "merely going through a stage," we need to bear in mind that the pressures are intense and the pain is real. For our children, adolescence is not simply a stage in their lives—it *is* their lives. In 1999, one out of every five adolescents had seriously considered suicide, and one out of ten had attempted it.

Being an adolescent *boy* in America also includes the extra burden associated with growing up in a culture of honor. The role models for adolescent boys in America are rough, tough heroes who are adept with weapons and fists—not wit. If you are an adolescent boy, you would be inclined to identify with John Wayne, Arnold Schwartzenegger, or Clint Eastwood, not Woody Allen. If you happen to be small and skinny and lack the ability to fight, you often find yourself in a situation involving the Hobson's choice of fight or flight.

If you pick up almost any textbook on adolescent psychology, you will find a statement similar to the one I found in an excellent book by Kathleen Berger. The statement appears as a caption under a photo of several bigger boys shoving around a smaller boy:

> The small, skinny boy seems overwhelmed by the horde towering around him, and he seems to be the target. . . . Many similarly built boys his age have already beat a shameful exit to the library, the TV, or their own private retreats.

In other words, the author, an expert on adolescence, accurately describes adolescence as a time punctuated by verbal and physical abuse, bullying, and shame. I am in total agreement with Dr. Berger's description. Indeed, as you will see when you read the next chapter, I was one of those skinny kids that Berger was writing about. I would raise one question: Is the skinny kid's humiliation inevitable? I don't think so. There are specific actions we can take to change that climate of humiliation, rejection, and the "shameful exit to the library." But before we can begin to do that, we must move beyond pump-handle solutions. We must make sure that we understand the root cause of the problem. For that, we must turn to the next chapter.

4

DEALING WITH DISASTERS: PART 2

The Importance of Root Cause Interventions

Dr. John Snow stopped the London cholera epidemic in 1854 by simply removing the pump handle from the wellhead, but he did not sit back and rest on his laurels. He realized that there was another step to be taken—that there was important information to be learned by figuring out how the well water got contaminated in the first place. Eventually, he discovered that fecal matter from nearby latrines had been seeping into that well for some time. It was likely, he reasoned, that all over England (and perhaps in most other parts of the world) latrines were being built too close to the existing supply of drinking water and that fecal matter might therefore leak into drinking water, causing cholera and other serious illnesses—illnesses that might be less dramatic and therefore less easily detectable than cholera. By finding the root cause of the contamination, he was able to instigate changes in building codes and their enforcement. This succeeded in preventing future outbreaks of cholera and generally improved the health and welfare of millions of people.

There is an important lesson to be learned here. Chapter 3 discussed installing metal detectors as one way to reduce the number of killings in schools. Such a draconian solution would have a myriad of psychological costs, but it would be fairly effective. If that is all we wanted to accomplish, we could install the metal detectors, sit back, and relax—more or less. There would be a diminution of mass murders in schools; I am certain of that.

But, of course, the root cause of the rash of mass murders in our schools is not the lack of metal detectors. The analogy with the cholera epidemic is an apt one. Just as it was essential for Dr. Snow to move beyond the pump handle, it is essential for us to understand what is causing these mass murders. It is reasonably clear that a major root cause of the recent school shootings is a school atmosphere that ignores, or implicitly condones, the taunting, rejection, and verbal abuse to which a great many students are subjected. A school that ignores the values of empathy, tolerance, and compassion—or, worse still, pays lip service to these values while doing nothing concrete and effective to promote these values—creates an atmosphere that is not only unpleasant for the "losers," but one that short changes the "winners" as well.

After the massacre, Columbine High School was depicted in the media in a most unflattering way. The charge was that the social atmosphere at Columbine was particularly unpleasant. It was suggested that the administration showed favoritism toward its athletes who dominated the school, that bullying and taunting were more prevalent at Columbine than at other schools, and that the administrators tolerated it. Understandably, the Columbine principal, several of the teachers, and many of the students were justifiably upset by this characterization. They maintained that Columbine was no different than most American schools. I can understand their upset and I sympathize with it. I also agree with their basic assertion. My best guess is that Columbine is no worse in this regard than most other schools.

Ironically, students attempting to defend themselves against this depiction made statements that bolstered my contention: Most members of the "in-group" consider taunting "outsiders" a reasonable thing to do. For example, after the content of the videotapes made by Harris and Klebold was made public, here is what one student, a member of the Columbine football team, had to say:

"Columbine is a good clean place except for those rejects. Most kids didn't want them there. They were into witchcraft. They were into voodoo. Sure we teased them. But what do you expect with kids who come to school with weird hairdos and horns on their hats? It's not just jocks; the whole school's disgusted with them. They're a bunch of homos, grabbing each other's private parts. If you want to get rid of someone, usually you tease 'em. So the whole school would call them homos, and when they did something sick, we'd tell them, 'You're sick and that's wrong.'"

In other words, Harris and Klebold were seen as "losers," so the "winners" felt justified in vilifying and taunting them. The quote also implies that Harris and Klebold were the only students being taunted, but I doubt that. It is hard to believe that Harris and Klebold were the only targets in a school atmosphere where taunting is so easily condoned. The underlying message of this student's statement is that rejection, name-calling, and taunting are part and parcel of the high school experience. I agree with him.

A further implication is that any students who dress in a way that is different from the norm, wear their hair differently, or behave differently have earned the disgust of the more traditional students and *deserve* to be teased, taunted, and rejected. That is where I disagree. We can do better than that. We can find a way to teach students a greater compassion for and tolerance of students who are different. We can even teach students to appreciate these differences and to experience them as sources of joy and excitement, rather than as automatic triggers for aggression and rejection.

Unfortunately, given the atmosphere that currently prevails in most high schools, few adolescents are immune to the social stresses of being a student. I know something about these stresses from personal experience. After all, I was once a high school student. Although many of my memories are positive, some of the most powerful are incredibly painful. One of my most vivid memories popped up when I read the caption of a photo taken in a high school that was profiled in Kathleen Berger's book—the photo I described in the preceding chapter. As you will recall, the caption read:

> The small, skinny boy seems overwhelmed by the horde towering around him, and he seems to be the target. . . . Many similarly built boys his age have already beat a shameful exit to the library, the TV, or their own private retreats.

When I was 16 years old, I was about 5' 10" tall but only weighed in at about 120 pounds, soaking wet. I could have posed for one of those "skinny-on-the-beach" ads that frequented the backs of comic books. You know the ads: The big, strong, muscular guy was forever kicking sand in the skinny kid's face and taking his girlfriend away from him. But then (in the next panel), the skinny kid sends away for the Charles Atlas bodybuilding course and, after a few months, he turns the tables on his tormentor and punches his lights out. I never sent away for the course, but once I almost succeeded in turning the tables on Tommy Foster.

Tommy Foster wasn't very smart or very charming—but he was extremely popular; he played middle linebacker on our high school football team. He was about my height—but was built like a fire hydrant—and was just as tough. He also seemed to have an extra supply of adrenaline coursing through his veins. He walked through high school with a swagger and a sneer. For reasons I never understood, he took an instant dislike to me and lost no opportunity to tell me about it. Tommy was a man of few words. His way of telling me about his animosity was to bounce a basketball off the back of my head during a lull in gym class, or to shove me hard in the back while I was standing in line in the cafeteria. When I turned in annoyance to see what had happened, there was Tommy grinning and snarling, "Whatcha gonna do about it? Ya wanna meet me outside afta skool?" Somehow, I got the idea that he didn't want to meet for a friendly chat. I always declined—trying, in vain, to make a joke out of it in order to save a little face while backing off. But I knew it was a no-win situation. As any man who has survived adolescence will attest, it is just about impossible to back away from a fight without losing face.

One day, while changing classes, I was walking beside a pretty girl whom I was trying to impress, when Tommy shoved his way between us, winked at the girl, slammed me hard against the wall, and kept on walking at a fast clip. The girl stopped in her tracks, and her mouth dropped open in bewilderment. The expression on her face seemed to be saying, "How can you allow him to do this to you? What kind of a man are you?" Seeing the situation through her eyes, I suddenly was overcome by feelings of humiliation and rage. Without thinking, I took off after Tommy Foster at full speed and yelled his name. He turned, just as I reached him. I lowered my shoulder and it caught him in the belly. We both went down hard, rolled over a couple of times, and, miraculously, I landed on top of him.

I would like to report that I emerged victorious like that other skinny kid—the one in the Charles Atlas ads. But I'm afraid that kind of thing mostly happens in those ads. In reality, when I knocked Tommy over, the element of surprise was useful—for about five seconds. During that small window of opportunity, I managed to get off one pretty good punch before Tommy grabbed the front of my shirt and pushed me over as if I were a rag doll. He then sat on my chest and, still holding firmly to my shirt with his left hand, sent his right fist crashing into my face three or four times.

Before others could intervene, my face was covered with blood. My physical pain was intense, but it was nothing compared to the humiliation I felt then—and for months to come. I became known as the kid who got punched out by Tommy Foster. Some kids taunted me about it. Others smirked when they talked to me. Most kept away from me as if I were some sort of a leper.

For the next few weeks, I had fantasies of somehow becoming bigger, stronger, and more adept with my fists, of challenging Tommy Foster to a fight, and of winning that fight with all the kids looking on with admiration. In my fantasy, they lifted me to their shoulders in triumph and I became the school hero. Reality was much harsher. I simply continued to go to school every day, trying hard to put the incident behind me and to stay out of Tommy Foster's way.

That incident took place more than fifty years ago but I still remember it vividly. Conventional wisdom holds that no one likes a bully. There may be some truth in that. But in my experience, my fellow students seemed perfectly happy to be hanging out with a bully like Tommy Foster— as long as he wasn't bullying *them!* It was only the targets of bullies that seemed to earn the taunts and disdain of other students.

The unfortunate thing is that the social situation in high schools hasn't changed that much in the past fifty years. Developmental psychologists who specialize in the study of adolescence tell us that my experience was far from unique. Bullying, taunting, ostracism, put-downs, sneering, and jeering are the norm. It is part of the general atmosphere of middle school and high school—at least for boys.

This raises several interesting questions. The first is: Why? Why do boys treat one another that way? Is it an essential aspect of being a young male? Is it biologically hardwired, having to do with a sharp increase in testosterone, or is it due to some form of social learning? Can it be changed? Could my high school have instituted policies that would have made the experience a more pleasant one for me—and for everybody else?

THE PREVALENCE OF CLIQUES

High school has always been dominated by cliques and these cliques are organized into a rough kind of hierarchy: athletes, cheerleaders, and social leaders near the top; the shy, inept or strange-acting kids near the bottom; and at the very bottom, the loners—those who don't seem to have any friends at all.

A Tale of Three Cities.

It would be instructive to take a close look at the social climate in a few high schools in different parts of the country to see if there are any similarities. Fortunately such data are readily available. A few months after the Columbine massacre, *Time* magazine visited a school in the center of our nation, Webster Groves High School in a suburb of St. Louis. The editors of *Time* magazine chose this particular high school because it exists in the geographical area in which values and attitudes seem to typify what is normative in the nation as a whole. To be specific, the editors say they chose Webster Groves:

> For the same reason marketing experts and sociologists like to wander this way when they are looking to take the country's temperature: The state of Missouri, especially the regions around St. Louis, are bellwether communities, not cutting edge, not

lagging indicators, but the middle of the country, middle of the road, middle of the sky.

Two weeks after the Columbine massacre, *The New York Times*, sent a reporter to examine the atmosphere in a high school in Scottsdale, Arizona. And, around the same time, in my hometown of Santa Cruz, California, the local newspaper sent its star reporter to interview a wide range of students from the area high schools as a way of gaining insight into the prevailing atmosphere. There is an amazing similarity in the ways that students in each of the three school districts sorted themselves out.

At Webster Groves, students are deeply cognizant of the "tribes" that form the basis of their social lives. At the top of the hierarchy are the jocks (the varsity athletes) and "The Clique." The Clique consists of students who have been friends since sixth grade and are involved in student government, theatre, and other highly visible activities. Outsiders say that these two groups "own the school." Further down in the hierarchy are the "technology twerps" and the so-called "in-between" crowd. At the bottom of the pecking order are the Church Step Dirties, who meet on the steps of a nearby church to smoke after school. More generally, at Webster Groves students get the most social points for having either a lot of athletic ability or a lot of money. They get the least points for opting out of the social system by looking weird and not caring about popularity.

Moving westward, one finds roughly the same hierarchy dominating Chaparral High School in Scottsdale, Arizona. The social geography at Chaparral is so clearly mapped out that it looks like an intentional design. But it's not. It's simply the way the students group themselves. Nevertheless, the groupings are clear and inviolable. At lunchtime, the athletes and their friends have the center table outdoors. In back of that table are some picnic tables occupied by students of slightly less important social status. Here one finds an array of cheerleaders, well-dressed preppies, and members of the student government.

> "You wouldn't dare come sit out here if you didn't know the people," said Lauren Barth, a sophomore cheerleader. "But once you're in with the girls, everyone is really friendly to you. When I made cheerleader, it was like I was just set."

At Chaparral, when you move from the prestigious outdoor tables to the inside of the cafeteria, you immediately notice that a lot more of the students are wearing eyeglasses, braces on their teeth, and hair that looks like it has never been carefully styled. These are clearly the students with less social status. These students are frequently referred to (by the others) as nerds. Still further down the hierarchy, there are students who seem to have no particular place. They are usually found eating upstairs or alone outside the library, or just wandering around, their eyes cast downward as they pass by clusters of their more popular schoolmates.

Continuing to move westward, to the coastal town of Santa Cruz, California, the students had no difficulty naming the cliques and indicating which of them each of their classmates fell into. In descending order of importance, there are the jocks, the preppies, the surfers, the roamers, the nerds, the goths, and the dirts. Aside from the fact that there were no "surfers" in St. Louis or Scottsdale (because there is no ocean!), one finds an eerie similarity between the "tribes" at Webster Groves, the groupings in Scottsdale, and the cliques at the Santa Cruz high schools. During the interviews in Santa Cruz, many of the students confessed that they considered high school to be a veritable battlefield. Those near the bottom of the heap reported that when they wake up in the morning and head for school they experience acute anxiety, never knowing whether they will be called names, jostled, or sprayed with chocolate milk. Heading into the cafeteria, they don't know where to sit. They know from bitter experience that there are certain tables where they would be unwelcome. Some search, mostly in vain, for a friendly face or a warm greeting. "Many sit alone in the corners, their headphones an invisible shield against the taunts, their knees pulled up to their chests."

Precisely where a student falls on the clique hierarchy determines his or her level of stress and degree of happiness. Moreover, according to Carol Miller Lieber of Educators for Social Responsibility, students who see themselves as being outside the select group of "winners" have far more negative views of their school than those inside that charmed circle. Perhaps most important, as Lieber puts it, "the winners are a smaller group than we'd like to think, and high school life is very different for those who experience it as the losers. They become part of the invisible middle and suffer in silence, alienated and without any real connection."

It is not difficult to broaden this analysis beyond the confines of these three rather typical, middle-class high schools. Shortly after the Columbine massacre, a search of the Internet revealed some powerful feelings being expressed by teenagers across the country. The overwhelming majority of them described how awful it feels to be rejected and taunted by their more popular classmates. And many of them correctly guessed that Harris and Klebold must have had similar experiences of rejection and exclusion (this months before the contents of the Harris/Klebold videotapes were released). None of these teenagers condoned the shootings, but their Internet postings revealed a surprisingly high degree of understanding and empathy for the suffering that Harris and Klebold must have endured.

A typical Internet posting was written by a 16-year-old girl who said: "I know how they feel. Parents need to realize that a kid is not overreacting all the time they say that no one accepts them. Also, all of the popular conformists need to learn to accept everyone else. Why do they shun everyone who is different?"

Another student wrote: "It's like in my school, the preppier kids think they're just everything. People are constantly harassing each other because they're different."

Another wrote: "It hurts so much to be seen as different but I have learned to get over it and move on. I think that if we had no cliques or at least others weren't looked down on as much, there would not be a problem."

A 17-year-old wrote: "Hey, the kids say that they did this because they were constantly teased and I can understand where they are coming from and I think that what they did to all of those kids was wrong but a person can only take so much torture."

It is possible that the students posting these notes represent only a tiny percentage of the high school population—perhaps such a small percentage of malcontents that they're hardly worth worrying about. Or perhaps they are the weird ones that at least one principal (described in Chapter 1) urged his "normal" students to identify as potential shooters. But as the research reported by Carol Miller Lieber suggests, the anguish expressed by these students is neither rare, nor weird. It represents the deep and abiding feelings of a sizable proportion of teenagers in this country who are living in a situation of daily stress.

Similarly, James Garbarino, a psychologist who has made a special study of adolescent violence, concludes that a number of teenagers are in a constant state of inner turmoil. Although most adolescents are like dandelions in the sense that they will thrive if given half a chance, some are more like orchids. According to Garbarino, these youngsters did fine as children, while they were young enough to be nurtured by loving parents, but they often wilt when, as adolescents they are subjected to peer competition, bullying, and rejection, particularly in large, impersonal high schools. His research shows that while most of these fragile children do fine in early childhood, fifty percent have significant difficulties once they enter adolescence.

Acting out in the extreme manner that Harris and Klebold did is rare, but a great many teenagers have fantasies about finding a way (albeit, a less violent way) to avenge themselves on their tormentors. The existence of these fantasies would help account for the enormous popularity among teenagers of such films as *Revenge of the Nerds*, *My Bodyguard*, and *Back to the Future*—each of which has, as its central theme, the rising up of downtrodden high school students. In these films, the acts of revenge were relatively benign—and certainly nonlethal.

But several other revenge films have achieved great popularity over the past two decades—films where the acts of revenge were indeed lethal—films like *Carrie, The Rage: Carrie 2*, and *Heathers*. It is fashionable to blame Hollywood for the violence occurring in schools. And there is no doubt that violent films do have an impact on the viewers, but simply viewing a violent film, in and of itself, will not lead to violent behavior. There is always some additional impetus.

As I was writing this book, I looked up the movie *Heathers* (made in 1989), on an Internet movie database to refresh my memory. The Web site featured only one reaction from a moviegoer. It speaks directly to the point I am making and, in a sense, is even more disconcerting than the film itself.

> This movie changed me. I saw it for the first time in 1995. I was part of the popular crowd and I hated it, because all they would do was make fun of people less than them. I still hate it. I watched this movie at exactly the right time. It gave me the motivation to forget my goddam prep crew friends and find some real ones. I didn't kill them and make it look like a suicide or anything, but I got out. This year I finally told them all off. The morons didn't even realize who they were hurting and what they were doing. Anyway, I can completely relate to this movie and there are Heathers everywhere. A girl in the popular crowd actually was named Heather. They're all such

snobs and this movie gives people like me hope, that there are good people out there, it just takes courage to find them, even if they're right in front of your face. That didn't make sense, but all I'm saying is that every teen should see this movie. I don't know if adults could relate to it because I haven't gotten there yet. But if you watch this movie, I truly believe you will come out a changed person.

After viewing the videos made by Harris and Klebold, one of the Littleton police investigators was inclined to focus on one element—a segment of the video indicating a desire to gain fame as a result of their action: The killers spent a few minutes speculating about who might direct the film to be made of the massacre. There is no doubt that attaining some sort of fame (or infamy) was on the minds of the two shooters. But it is reasonably clear that fame was merely a secondary motive. Their primary motive, which they stated over and over again on the video, was to extract revenge—not simply from the specific students who might have caused them pain and humiliation, but from everyone in sight. "We're going to kick-start a revolution," Harris says, "a revolution of the dispossessed." The video also makes it clear that they were fully determined to take their own lives. This was part of the plan from the outset. Fame may have been on their minds, but they had no intention of being around to bask in it.

Interestingly enough, Harris's and Klebold's desire to avenge their feelings of humiliation bears a striking resemblance to the major motive underlying the behavior of adult murderers. James Gilligan, the director of psychiatric services for the Massachusetts State Prison System, spent over a decade working closely with a wide range of male killers. The experience convinced him that virtually all killers share an overwhelming sense of shame brought on by rejection and humiliation. According to Gilligan, their violent behavior toward others is an attempt to replace shame with pride, an attempt to gain the respect that they felt was being withheld from them. Gilligan's analysis (published several years prior to the Columbine massacre) is eerily confirmed by the videotapes Harris and Klebold left behind: "Isn't it fun finally to get the respect that we are going to deserve?" asks Harris, clutching the sawed-off shotgun he was about to use against his classmates.

THE FALLACY OF PUMP-HANDLE INTERVENTIONS

Armed guards and metal detectors will probably reduce the number of multiple shootings in our schools, but they will not reduce the magnitude of the problems that are at the root of the shootings. They will not make school a happier place for the students who feel excluded, rejected, and humiliated. Identifying the youngsters who are most hurt by having been excluded—either by asking other students to point them out and turn them in, or by forcing them to take some sort of personality test—will not solve the problem. Indeed, singling out these youngsters is likely to exacerbate the root problem by increasing their level of exclusion. Moreover, personality tests simply are not as accurate or as precise as the general public thinks they are. Attempts to identify troubled youngsters with such tests will undoubtedly target a great many who are not troubled at all, while allowing some seriously troubled individuals to slip by undetected.

But even if the personality tests were 100 percent accurate, it is simply the wrong approach to the problem. A recent FBI analysis of the recent school shootings suggests that many schools are overreacting by searching for troubled teenagers or by suspending students for minor infractions under the new zero-tolerance policies. The FBI analysis concludes that most students who shoot their classmates are not maladjusted loners. Most were doing well academically, and had not been identified by school officials as problem students.

The FBI has compiled a list of fifty risk factors, and the Bureau of Alcohol, Tobacco, and Firearms has developed computer software, to help schools identify potential student killers. But all of the attention that is focused on ferreting out school shooters before they create another tragedy has obscured the fact that these killings take place at school. Young mass murderers don't mow down their neighbors or shoot up the local video arcade. They kill their classmates and teachers, and sometimes themselves, in or around the school building itself. Looking for root causes in individual pathology is an approach that seems sensible on the surface, but it does not get to the root of the problem. What is it about the atmosphere in the schools themselves that makes these young people so desperate, diabolical, and callous? Why do they seek revenge, or a twisted notion of glory, by shooting their classmates? In what ways have they felt rejected, ignored, humiliated, or treated unfairly at school? Are schools doing the best they can to develop students' characters as well as their intellects? Can schools do better at creating inclusive, caring communities with positive role models for students?

Schools are falling down on the job if they allow a large proportion of the student body to be made miserable by exclusion and ostracism. This would be a problem even if there had never been a single shooting. The shootings are tragic and need to be prevented, of course, but at the same time, the shootings serve to alert us to the underlying problem. By finding a solution to the underlying problem, we will succeed not only in making our schools safer, but we will also make them happier and more humane places for all of the students. In the next two chapters, we will look at some strategies for getting to the root of the problem and affecting a real change in the atmosphere of our schools.

5

ROOT CAUSE INTERVENTIONS, PART 1

Can't We All Just Get Along?

> When a human being experiences himself, his thoughts
> and feelings as separated from the rest of humankind, it
> is a kind of optical delusion of consciousness. This delu-
> sion is a prison, restricting us to our personal desires
> and to affection for the few persons nearest us. Our task
> must be to free ourselves from this prison by widening
> our circle of compassion, to embrace all living creatures
> and the whole of nature in its beauty. Nobody is able to
> achieve this completely, but the striving for such an
> achievement is, in itself, a part of the liberation and
> foundation of our inner security.
>
> —ALBERT EINSTEIN

A lot of learning takes place in school. Some of it is academic, but much of it is implicit. By "implicit" I mean
things that aren't taught, but that are learned nevertheless.

So what social lessons do youngsters learn by hanging out in the schoolyard, the cafeteria, and the corridors? Unfortunately, many learn that the world is a difficult, unfriendly place. Many learn that the law of the jungle prevails, that might makes right, that they are on their own, and that they can't look to adults to help solve their personal problems. Many learn that they are unattractive and unpopular, that others do not want them around.

When our teenage children come home from school agonizing over a problem they are having with their classmates, there may be a tendency for us to shrug and say to ourselves, "That's just high school." But, as I indicated earlier, to teenagers, high school is not simply a passing phase in their lives; it *is* their lives! It is also the living laboratory in which adolescents learn how to relate to other people. The sad fact is that a great many teenagers are unhappy in high school because they are excluded, taunted, and lonely. They become anxious and depressed; their schoolwork suffers; their self-esteem plummets. A small percentage act out in horrific ways. Among teenagers, extreme unhappiness, depression, and serious thoughts of suicide are not rare. The latest government figures are chilling: They show that in 1999 one out of every five adolescents had seriously considered suicide, and one out of ten had attempted it. This represents an increase of some four hundred percent since 1950. It would be a serious mistake for parents to think of this unhappiness as minor or to attribute it to the inevitability of being a teenager. It is not minor and it is not inevitable.

Can the general social climate of exclusion that exists in our schools be changed? Can youngsters be taught compassion and empathy for other human beings? Can they be taught specific ways of living happily and productively with different kinds of people without excluding them, without putting them down, without humiliating them? As Rodney King once lamented, "Can't we all just get along?"

We all know that, at its best, schools can teach students to master a variety of academic subjects from Shakespeare to calculus. Unfortunately, most parents and some school administrators believe that teaching basic academic skills should be the only mission of schools. I think that belief is shortsighted. Our schools can and should play a vital role in helping students develop emotional mastery as well as academic mastery. A school's social climate can do a great deal to either foster or hinder a student's skill in getting along with others. Schools can create a learning environment that not only deters violence, but also educates young people in emotional maturity and emotional intelligence. I believe that this is not only a worthwhile goal but that it is also vital for a youngster's full development.

Moreover, as an extra bonus, it is becoming increasingly clear that such an education has market value. Most corporations are now looking for employees who are not only good at the mastery of a particular set of academic skills but who also have the ability to work harmoniously with a wide variety of coworkers as a cooperative team, to demonstrate initiative and responsibility, and to communicate effectively. Corporations spend millions of dollars on workshops that teach teamwork and tolerance for diversity. They realize that it is not only politically correct, that it not only creates a happy work environment, but that it is also good for the bottom line.

WHAT IS EMOTIONAL INTELLIGENCE?

We all have some idea what is meant by the term "intelligence" or "IQ." Somebody with a high IQ has a wide and deep general knowledge, as well as the ability to solve a variety of mathematical and verbal problems. These individuals learn quickly and usually perform well on exams and quiz shows. But what do we mean by the term "emotional intelligence"? As social psychologist Daniel Goleman puts it, emotional intelligence is a person's ability to be aware of, and to control, his own emotions. It involves the development of self-restraint and compassion in dealing with others, the ability to motivate oneself and to work with passion and persistence.

I know what emotional intelligence means in practice. I have been teaching young people at colleges and universities for more than forty years. A small percentage of my students are a pleasure to teach right from the beginning. They are eager to learn, work diligently, participate in class discussions, and ask interesting and thoughtful questions. They are cooperative and helpful in discussion groups. They listen attentively and respond thoughtfully to their classmates. If they get a disappointing grade on a paper, they come back to my office to see me and ask what they did wrong and how they can improve. At the other end of the continuum are students who seem to lack these abilities entirely. They can't seem to get it together; they whine about assignments, make excuses, and complain of unfairness. Some of these students are very bright, but difficult and unrewarding to deal with. They simply don't have what it takes to get their assignments done smoothly and work harmoniously with others.

The developmental psychologist Howard Gardner takes the concept of emotional intelligence a step further, suggesting that it may be more important than what is traditionally referred to as IQ. Gardner also suggests that two kinds of intelligence can fit under the general rubric of emotional intelligence. One of these can be called *intrapersonal intelligence*—a talent for understanding oneself. The other can be called *interpersonal intelligence*—a talent for getting along well with other people. These are recognized by Gardner as key life skills. As Gardner puts it: "Many people with IQs of 160 work for people with IQs of 100, if the former have poor intrapersonal intelligence and the latter have a high one. And in the day-to-day world no intelligence is more important than the interpersonal. If you don't have it, you'll make poor choices about whom to marry, what job to take, and so on. We need to train children in the personal intelligences in school."

From all the evidence I can gather, it seems that Harris and Klebold had above-average academic IQs, but they were sadly lacking in emotional intelligence. The videotapes they left behind show them brooding over every slight, every

insult. They also show them nursing their righteous indigna-
tion and feeding the anger they harbored against their fellow
students. Who was at fault? It is not an either/or situation:
Yes, they were almost certainly treated shabbily; and yes, they
were not equipped to deal with that shabby treatment in a
reasonable way. Unfortunately, not many teenagers are.

HOW IMPORTANT IS EMOTIONAL INTELLIGENCE?

Let us look briefly at research that tests a crucial aspect of
emotional intelligence: the ability of young children to
resist temptation and delay gratification. Beginning in the
1960s, social psychologist Walter Mischel devised a simple
but ingenious set of experiments to test this ability. In a typical experiment, Mischel brought 4-year-old children into a
room, one at a time, and seated them at a table. On the table
was a marshmallow. Mischel informed the child that he
could eat the marshmallow immediately, or, if he waited a
little while, he could have two marshmallows. Mischel then
left the room and kept the kids waiting for fifteen to twenty
minutes. As you might imagine, this was a difficult task for
most four-year olds. Alone in a room with nothing to do but
look at the marshmallow, the temptation to eat it was great.
Indeed, it was too great for about one-third of the children.
They couldn't resist gobbling up the marshmallow. About
two-thirds of the children managed to delay gratification so
that they could get the greater reward. Some were able to
distract themselves for the entire fifteen to twenty minutes
by covering their eyes, singing to themselves, inventing

games, or using other diversionary tactics. Even at age 4, they already had the capacity to control their impulse to eat a sweet treat immediately.

Now, here's what I regard as the most interesting part of the experiment: A dozen years later, Mischel and his colleagues restudied these same children and found remarkable differences between those who had been able to delay gratification and those who had not. By and large, as 16-year-olds, those who had been able to delay gratification at age 4 were more confident, self-assured, trustworthy, dependable, willing to take the initiative and plunge into projects, and less likely to fall apart in the face of disappointment or difficulty than those who could not delay gratification at age 4. At age 16, they were still able to delay immediate gratification and keep their eyes on their long-term goals. The young people who, at age 4, ate the marshmallow immediately were more likely to feel bad about themselves, to be troubled, stubborn, indecisive, short-tempered, jealous, resentful, easily upset by frustration, and immobilized by stress.

There may be a genetic component to this ability, but it is reasonably clear that delaying gratification is primarily learned. I say this because research has pointed to some powerful situational factors that determine which 4-year-olds will have developed this ability. One important factor is whether the child has siblings close in age. Two- or 3-year-olds with a baby sister or baby brother will not always get what they want when they want it. Accordingly, by the time they are 4, they will have had a lot of practice waiting for things. This speculation is confirmed by research showing that twins and triplets tend to have the most highly developed ability to delay gratification.

Judging by the behavior of Harris and Klebold as teenagers, I would speculate that they would have been among those 4-year-old children who couldn't wait to eat the marshmallow. However smart they were in the academic realm, they were unable to withstand the slings and arrows of high school social life. Why? Maybe they were, temperamentally, the fragile "orchid" types that I described earlier. Or perhaps, like most other boys, they felt the kind of pressure that I felt as a skinny teenager when I tried to retaliate against Tommy Foster, the pressure to measure up to the cultural ideal of manhood.

THE BOY CODE

Like any parent, I know that boys and girls are different. I also know that the differences show up in early childhood. Give almost any little boy a doll and he'll turn it into an imaginary weapon or vehicle; give almost any little girl a toy truck and she'll wrap it in a blanket and cuddle it in her arms. Developmental psychologists may disagree about the extent to which genetics or social learning affects this behavior, but they are in total agreement about the behavior itself. Is it any wonder that girls seem to end up with a more generous measure of emotional intelligence than boys? Dozens of studies have found that females are more empathic than males and better able to read others' emotions. As they go through elementary school, girls become more emotionally expressive, boys less so. Instead, boys build up a wall of emotional toughness as they become skilled at downplaying their feelings of vulnerability, guilt, fear, and hurt.

It is important to note that boys and girls do not start life far apart on this dimension. In fact, there is some evidence that baby boys are more emotionally expressive than baby girls. What starts to happen, even in infancy, says psychologist William Pollack, is that parents, schools, and society train boys out of emotional intelligence. All conspire unwittingly to enforce what Pollack calls the Boy Code, an unwritten set of guidelines for male behavior:

1. The "sturdy oak." Boys should be stoic and never show weakness. As one boy explained, "If somebody slugs you in the face, probably the best thing you could do is just smile and act like it didn't hurt. You definitely shouldn't cry or say anything."

2. "Give 'em hell." Macho movie characters and sports coaches encourage young males to act tough and dare each other to engage in risky feats. Males gain peer status through successfully completing a dare.

3. The "big wheel." The imperative to achieve dominance, status, and power, to wear a mask of coolness, to pretend

everything is going fine, even if it isn't, often impels males to push themselves hard to achieve and to repress feelings of inadequacy.

4. "No sissy stuff." Boys are ridiculed and taunted if they express "feminine" or vulnerable feelings. The only socially acceptable emotional expression for males becomes anger.

Boys absorb these injunctions at home, on TV, on the playground, at school, and seem to fear breaking them. Expressions such as "real boys don't cry," "don't be a sissy," "don't be a crybaby," "be a man," and "be tough" reinforce the image of masculinity presented to boys. As a result, says Pollack, males are "living with half the self—the heroic self," and are robbed of the chance to experience a full emotional life.

By all accounts, Harris and Klebold (like all the recent teenage killers) followed the Boy Code to the end. They endured taunting and humiliation "like a man," reacting not with tears but with anger. They kept their cool in public, never admitting their feelings of shame and anguish to their parents, teachers, or (in Harris's case) therapist. And, in the end, they "gave 'em hell." Indeed, for these two misguided young men, their desire for revenge and respect was more important than their own lives.

This is a sadly familiar scenario. When news of yet another school shooting comes across the airwaves, one part of the story that does not surprise us is that the person pulling the trigger is a male. Violence is by and large a male problem, both for adolescents and adults. A recent analysis by the U.S. Justice Department revealed that males commit six times as many violent crimes as females and that males commit far more serious violent crimes. The implications of this difference are stunning: "There is one violent male offender for every nine males age 10 and older compared with one violent female offender for every fifty-six women age 10 and older." The roots of violent behavior are surely in the society at large. But when violence occurs at schools, it is a problem that schools must deal with and ultimately prevent.

WHY IS THIS THE SCHOOLS' PROBLEM?

Aren't we asking too much of schools? These days parents and politicians are pushing our nation's schools to produce better-educated students who can pass standardized proficiency exams. They are pressuring teachers to focus on the basics and forget the frills. The crucial question is: What constitutes a frill? My concern is that in their zeal to get back to basics policy makers may be losing sight of how crucial the social climate of a school can be in the lives of young people. How connected youngsters feel at school is an important factor in protecting them from extreme emotional distress, drug abuse, and violence. In fact, young males are often most prone to become violent when they sense that an important social connection is eroding, whether with their family, a girlfriend, or their school.

Psychologist James Garbarino, who studies young male criminals, points out that boys who kill at school still care about school. This is not only a rather touching finding, but it is also an important clue. Boys who kill are not the boys who have dropped out (physically or emotionally), joined gangs, or gone to jail. Rather, they are the boys who want a connection with their school. I think it is important to underscore the obvious: It is unfortunate that it takes a tragedy like the Columbine shootings to call our attention to the ways a school can change a stressful social climate into a more accepting one.

Is this an unreasonable goal? I don't think so. Let us look at the issue of depression—an illness that Eric Harris was being treated for at the time of the massacre. As we have seen, depression is not uncommon among adolescents. Psychiatrists and psychologists are fairly adept at treating this illness once it occurs. But why wait for something to be broken before attempting to fix it? Schools can play a crucial role in the *prevention* of depression.

Administrators at an Oregon high school grew concerned that some twenty-five percent of their student body showed early signs of depression. So they initiated a special program aimed at developing certain aspects of emotional intelligence they thought might be helpful in dealing with depression. They randomly placed seventy-five of these at-risk students in a special course that met regularly after the close of the usual school day. The course, consisting of only eight one-hour sessions, focused on helping the students learn strategies that would enable them to get along better with their parents and peers. The results were encouraging. More than half of the students in the class recovered from their mild depression, compared with only a quarter of similar students who did not participate in the class. A year later, only fourteen percent of the students who had participated in the depression-prevention program fell into a major depression, compared to twenty-five percent of those who had not been in the program. What excites me about this program is that such a minor intervention (only eight sessions) produced significant long-term effects, nearly cutting in half the number of students who eventually suffered a full-blown depression.

So we know that relatively simple programs can help prevent vulnerable students from falling into a serious depression. This is a worthwhile goal in and of itself, but it isn't the only incentive for schools to focus on their students' emotional intelligence. It turns out that learning strategies of emotional intelligence is not only good for students' mental health, it is also good for a school's bottom line—academic achievement. No matter how you look at it, higher emotional intelligence means higher academic achievement. The marshmallow kids are a prime example. Mischel and his colleagues went back and studied these youngsters for a third time as they were finishing high school. Those who had the skill to delay gratification at age 4 were more competent academically at age 18. They were more eager to learn, better able to reason, and better able to organize and express their ideas. Their SAT scores were also dramatically higher (by an average of 210 points!) than the scores of the students who acted impulsively as children and immediately ate the marshmallow. It is important to mention that the ability to delay gratification is not highly correlated with IQ. In fact, the children's performance on the marshmallow test was twice as powerful a predictor of their SAT scores as was their IQ. Other studies have also demonstrated that emotional intelligence (EQ) and academic intelligence (IQ) are separate qualities, and that emotional intelligence is a better predictor of success in school.

ACTIVELY REDUCING BULLYING AND TAUNTING

In the wake of the Columbine tragedy, many schools instituted zero-tolerance policies for weapons, for drugs, and, sometimes, for fighting. In my opinion, schools should make a similar kind of serious attempt to reduce or eliminate bullying, taunting, and insulting behavior. It is astonishing to me that we permit children to be victimized by the kind of verbal violence that adults would not tolerate in their own workplace. Indeed, in many instances, adults subjected to such harassment would sue not only the perpetrator, but also their employer for allowing such an intolerable work environment.

Why the difference between what is tolerated in the adult work-world and the adolescent work-world? My educated guess is that the general public implicitly believes that teasing and bullying are part of growing up, a kind of developmental gauntlet that children and adolescents must learn to endure and deal with. But the consequences of bullying can be serious. Many adults (myself included) bear the emotional scars of having been bullied in school. I survived the experience, but the bullying incident was traumatic at the time and still rankles some fifty years later. I certainly wouldn't want my grandchildren to experience that kind of stress. I still can't help thinking that the school could have done more to prevent that kind of situation. This would have been helpful not only to me, but to Tommy Foster as well. Research shows that the outcome for bullies is usually worse than for their victims. I don't know what ever became of Tommy Foster. I wish him no harm, but the odds are against him. Research shows that whatever pleasure he derived from being top dog in high school probably didn't serve him well in adult life. Bullies tend to become more hostile over time, losing the support and admiration of their peers as they grow up and frequently getting into serious trouble. One study found that by age 24 two-thirds of boys who were bullies in elementary school had been convicted of at least one felony. One-third of the boys who were bullies in middle school had been convicted of three or more crimes, often violent ones, and had already done prison time. Thus, allowing students to bully one another in school is akin to giving aggressive children training for a life of crime.

But it doesn't have to be that way. A remarkable effort to investigate and curb bullying took place in virtually the entire country of Norway. It began with the Norwegian government's concern over the suicides of three young victims of bullying. Typical is the case of "Henry," who didn't quite succeed in taking his own life:

> On a daily basis, Henry's classmates called him "Worm," broke his pencils, spilled his books on the floor, and mocked him whenever he answered a teacher's questions. Finally, a few boys took him to the bathroom and made him lie, facedown, in the urinal drain. After school that day he tried to kill himself. His parents found him unconscious, and only then learned about his torment.

At the request of the government, psychologist Dan Olweus surveyed all of Norway's 90,000 schoolchildren. Olweus concluded that bullying was serious and widespread. In some schools, as many as seventeen percent of the students reported being continually harassed by bullies. He also found that teachers and parents were only dimly aware of bullying incidents, and that even when adults were aware of these incidents they rarely intervened.

The Norwegian government sponsored a three-tiered campaign in every school to change the social dynamic that breeds bullies and victims. First, community-wide meetings were held to explain the problem. Parents were given brochures detailing symptoms of victimization. Teachers received special training on recognizing and dealing with bullying. Students watched videotapes designed to evoke empathy and sympathy for victims of bullying.

On a second level, classes discussed specific ways to prevent bullying and befriend socially isolated or lonely children. Teachers organized cooperative learning groups and moved quickly to stop name-calling and other aggression that escalates into bullying. Principals ensured that lunchrooms, bathrooms, and playgrounds were adequately supervised.

A third set of measures came into play if bullying occurred despite these preventive steps. Counselors conducted intensive therapy with the bully and his or her parents, and sometimes assigned the bully to a different class or school. They also helped the victim strengthen social and academic skills.

Twenty months after the campaign began, Olweus found that bullying overall had decreased by fifty percent, with significant improvements at every grade level. He concludes, "It is no longer possible to avoid taking action about bullying problems at school using lack of awareness as an excuse—it all boils down to a matter of will and involvement on the part of adults."

TEACHING STUDENTS THE SKILL OF GETTING ALONG

We don't expect students to learn algebra on their own, or to become good violinists or competent tennis players without instruction. Yet somehow we think that children can learn how to get along with each other merely by being thrown together at school. Some do, of course. But many more students would get along if schools made human relations a part of the curriculum. There are many ways of doing this, from teaching children to recognize and understand their emotions, to helping students develop greater empathy for others, to giving students the tools to resolve conflicts, to actively teaching students ways to make friends. I have often thought that learning some of the principles of social psychology would be useful to high school students in their daily lives.

Dealing with Our Emotions

Some schools are trying to give younger students these useful tools. For example, at Nueva Learning Center, a private school in California, students take a class called Self Science, in which they study about human emotions and learn how to deal with setbacks and interpersonal conflicts. The curriculum of the class—the tensions and traumas of students' everyday lives—is usually ignored by other schools: How do you feel when a friend no longer seems interested in you? What can you say to someone whose grandmother has just died? How can you approach a group that you want to join? How can you get someone to stop teasing you? How can you handle not making the football team or the debating squad? What do you do if friends try to get you to drink alcohol or use drugs? Through discussions and explorations of typical concerns such as these, students have become skilled in recognizing emotions in themselves and others, evaluating and choosing responses, and communicating with their peers.

Recognizing Emotions in Others

Teachers at an inner-city school in Connecticut have come to consider emotional intelligence a survival skill. Most of the students in this school come face-to-face with a dangerous environment on a daily basis. They live in neighborhoods plagued by drugs and violence. To help deal with this issue, the school's curriculum teaches emotional intelligence. One lesson simply involves being able to recognize another person's emotions by looking at his facial expression. Students look at pictures of faces expressing anger, fear, disgust, sadness, surprise, and happiness. They analyze how the mouth, eyes, eyebrows, and forehead change with different emotions. Recognizing the emotion on someone's face may seem obvious, not a skill that needs to be taught. But youngsters often get into trouble with one another because they misinterpret the emotional expressions of other people. For example, bullies often mistake another person's neutral expressions or comments for hostile attacks and will proceed to lash out in retaliation.

Resolving Conflicts Peacefully

One of the most challenging situations for educators entails resolving conflicts between students and preventing disagreements and minor altercations from escalating into violence. Schools take a variety of approaches to helping students develop the skills to work out disagreements. At Webster Groves High School, a mediation session takes place an average of once a day. Coming to mediation is voluntary, but there is an incentive: It can forestall a suspension. Under the direction of the assistant principal, specially trained staff members or students conduct a role-playing exercise in which each party in the conflict takes the other person's perspective, stating what the other person must have felt and thought during the incident. Being able to see the other party's point of view not only starts to defuse the anger generated by the particular conflict, it also expands students' ability to anticipate and interpret others' feelings, to think before acting, and to develop skills in discussing differences rather than fighting.

Some schools focus on helping students develop such skills from the earliest grades. At an elementary school in California, a daily community circle is the forum for discussing "good news" and "bad news" in every class. Even kindergartners become adept at saying to classmates, "I liked it when you played with me at recess" and "I didn't like it when I spilled my milk and you laughed at me. It made me feel bad." In this way, children get to air their grievances and work out their problems in a supportive atmosphere, while at the same time becoming aware of the emotional impact of their actions on others. If a conflict cannot be resolved easily within the circle, students can discuss the situation with each other privately—with the supervision and assistance of the teacher or a parent who has been trained in conflict resolution techniques.

At this same school, one of the most important tasks at the beginning of the school year is for the class to formulate a list of class agreements for acceptable behavior, along with consequences for misbehavior. The agreements are posted in the classroom and students refer to them in evaluating their own and others' behavior. This kind of democratic process operates in the school as a whole. When a third-grade boy was continually too aggressive in a ball-game on the playground, the principal came to the community circle in each third-grade class and listened to students' suggestions about how to deal with the problem. Students in one class came to the consensus that if the offender played too roughly he should not be allowed to play the game for two days.

A school in Seattle uses a similar approach to focusing on students' relationship problems. They have a mailbox in each classroom for student messages. A third-grade mailbox contained the following message—"My friends Alice and Lynn won't play with me." The teacher uses such a concern as a springboard for class discussion—with no names named—about the vicissitudes of friendship, how it feels to be left out, how relationships can change over time, how people can make new friends, and so on.

At the inner-city school in Connecticut mentioned above, teachers train students to think before they act. Once they have received serious training, various prompts are utilized to help students bring their training to mind and into clear focus. For example, one such device is the "stoplight" poster: In the heat of the moment, when tempers are flaring, glancing at a poster in the classroom can help students remember what they have learned about ways to control their emotional impulses. The "stoplight" poster has six steps:

Red light	1. Stop, calm down, and think before you act.
Yellow light	2. Say the problem and how you feel.
	3. Set a positive goal.
	4. Think of lots of solutions.
	5. Think ahead to the consequences.
Green light	6. Go ahead and try the best plan.

Another program, called Resolving Conflict Creatively, is used in several hundred New York City public schools, as well as schools across the country. The program involves classroom brainstorming exercises about alternatives to violence as well as having trained student mediators available on the playground to help resolve disputes. The focus of the program is on preventing violence, but teachers see broader benefits. The training in recognizing and under-

standing feelings improves students' emotional compe-
tence in general and leads to an increase in "caring among
the kids."

Special Problems of School Structure

These programs have proven successful at building greater
understanding of our own emotions and those of others.
Unfortunately, almost all of these programs were developed
particularly for elementary school–age children. Don't get
me wrong. I think this kind of learning is wonderful for
elementary schoolchildren. But what about middle school
and high school students? I can't help believing that if
the tension and conflicts between the goths and the jocks at
Columbine High School had been addressed openly in a
schoolwide forum, things might have turned out differently.

Here's the point: These programs are useful for students
of all ages. And it is clear to me that middle school and high
school students are actually in greater need of this kind
of guidance than younger children. Teenagers have to deal
with six different teachers and sets of classmates every day.
How would adults cope if they had to do that at their workplace? Instead, most adults' job environment is more like
an elementary school classroom; you deal with the same
predictable group of people in the same familiar space all
day. The structure of secondary schools serves to exacerbate, rather than alleviate, the feelings of insecurity that are
a natural part of adolescence.

What makes it worse is that high school students are treated in contradictory ways by their teachers. Sometimes they are treated as children and sometimes as adults. In their academic life, they are told what, when, and how to study. They are usually not expected to assume adult responsibility for their own intellectual development. At the same time, they are given virtually no guidance concerning their emotional development. Instead, they are pretty much left on their own and expected to work out their problems by themselves. It's no wonder that many of them could use some help in understanding and relating to each other. And the best place to do this is at school, among their peers.

DEVELOPING EMPATHY

Empathy is putting yourself in the shoes of another person to feel with that person, to gain an awareness and understanding of what that person must be feeling, and to identify your own feelings accurately and respond appropriately. If Brian comes to school looking uncharacteristically sad, an empathic fellow student like Dana will notice that Brian seems sad. When Brian says that his grandfather has just died, Dana will be able to imagine what it might be like to lose a beloved grandparent, to feel some of Brian's sadness, and to offer words of sympathy and comfort. Learning about the facial expressions of emotion, as students in the

Connecticut school do, is essentially a beginning lesson in empathy.

Why should schools be concerned with fostering empathy in students? Children who are more empathic tend to be more cooperative and less aggressive. Once a child has learned to put himself in the shoes of another person, it is very difficult to aggress against that person. If we have learned to put ourselves in the shoes of a great many other people, aggressive responses, in general, become less available to us.

Like other positive attributes, the learning of empathy has its beginnings in the home. Research indicates that the degree of empathy shown by young girls matches the degree of empathy shown by their own mothers toward them. Boys tend to be less influenced by their mothers' empathy, but one aspect of parenting is of great significance for boys: Boys tend to have low empathy if their parents put heavy emphasis on competition. This makes good sense; if you are hell-bent on winning, it helps if you do not concern yourself with your opponent's feelings. This kind of attitude may be useful for winning games, but an overconcern with competitiveness can produce some disastrous consequences, unless other steps are taken to foster the development of empathy. Fortunately, the home is not the only place where empathy can be learned. It can also be learned in school. In the classroom, empathy can either be taught directly or learned indirectly.

Teaching Empathy

"What would the world look like to you if you were as small as a cat?" "What birthday present would make each member of your family happiest?" These kinds of questions formed the basis of exercises for elementary school children in Los Angeles who participated in a thirty-hour program designed by psychologist Norma Feshbach to teach empathy. Thinking hard about the answers to such questions expands children's ability to put themselves in another's situation. In addition, the children listened to stories and then retold them from the point of view of each of the different characters in each story. The children played the role of each of the characters. The performances were videotaped. They then viewed the tapes and analyzed how people look and sound when they express different feelings.

At first glance, such a program may seem unrelated to academics. Yet the role-playing and close analysis of stories is just what high school and college students do in putting on a play or analyzing a piece of literature. Interestingly, in reminiscing about his childhood, the Nobel prize–winning physicist Richard Feynman reported that his father challenged his intellect by asking him to pretend he was a tiny creature living in their living room carpet. In order to deal with that challenge, Feynman needed, in effect, to crawl into the skin and persona of that tiny creature. Such questions also encourage the kind of "out-of-the-box" thinking and cognitive flexibility taught in corporate creativity programs. Accordingly, it should not surprise us when Norma Feshbach reports that students who have learned to develop greater empathic ability also tend to have higher academic achievement.

The children in Feshbach's program not only learned to be more empathic, but they also showed higher self-esteem, greater generosity, more positive attitudes, and less aggressiveness than students who had not participated in the program. Empathy can be taught. Some schools have managed to integrate empathy training with their students' regular academic curriculum. Feshbach has designed curriculum materials that guide high school teachers in teaching about the history of immigration to the U.S. The goal is to help students understand the perspectives of different groups of immigrants, empathize with their particular situation, and feel the painful consequences of the prejudice with which many groups were treated. It should be clear that students who study U.S. history using this approach have a better chance of becoming more tolerant of students from other ethnic groups at their own school, leading to an overall decrease in inter-ethnic hostility on campus.

DEALING WITH UNPOPULARITY

"No one will play with me" is a common childhood lament, but for some children it may be true. Some of the most painful experiences in a child's life involve being left out, rejected, or bullied by other children. A child who is unpopular because she lacks social skills will not have a chance to become more skilled if none of her peers will spend time with her. This unpopularity in childhood can have serious consequences in adulthood. Social psychologist Kip Williams has shown that the feelings of being ostracized by others in childhood can have long-term effects in terms of a serious reduction in self-esteem. And as Dan Goleman points out, "How popular a child was in third grade has been shown to be a better predictor of mental-health problems at age 18 than anything else—teachers' and nurses' ratings, school performance and IQ, even scores on psychological tests."

Children who are unpopular are lacking in emotional intelligence; they don't intuitively know how to relate well to other children. Some are too touchy, prone to take offense at the slightest provocation, quick to retaliate angrily. Others are too timid and anxious. Still others seem "off" to their peers; their interactions with others are awkward or inappropriate. Having at least one friend, even if the relationship is marginal, can mean all the difference in a young person's emotional development.

Again, one might legitimately ask whether it is the responsibility of schools to ensure that every student has a friend. Increasingly, some of our most eminent educators are emphatically saying *yes!* Ted and Nancy Sizer recently wrote, "Belonging is something that every adolescent should expect at a school. Belonging, or the right to belong, is a moral right of adolescence. And no matter how hard she might make it for us, it is not principled to allow an unformed young adult to be a loner, to be out of reach. We should shove ourselves into her life."

But how can schools best "shove their way" into a student's social life? It turns out that it is not that difficult. Even small, targeted programs can have a remarkable effect. Psychologist Steven Asher designed a series of six "friendship coaching" sessions, in which selected unpopular students in the third and fourth grades were taught to act in ways typical of more popular students. Some of the social rules that are second nature to most youngsters have somehow eluded these students. They are taught to say something nice when another youngster does well at a game or to remember to talk and ask questions when playing a game with someone. A year after the coaching sessions, the targeted students, selected because they were the least popular in their class, had moved up to the middle of the class popularity ranking.

Such programs have a fifty to sixty percent success rate in increasing the acceptance of rejected youngsters, and they seem to work best for third- and fourth-graders. But similar programs could be tailored to the needs of adolescents. These interventions do not need to be elaborate. Something as simple as assigning an upper-grade student to serve as a mentor to every incoming student would give anxious newcomers a head start on making social connections at school. Interestingly enough, Columbine High School has recently instituted this kind of mentoring program for newcomers.

USING TEAMWORK TO OVERCOME ANIMOSITY

As I suggested earlier, many adults seem to have the attitude that angst is part and parcel of adolescence, that emotional ups and downs are not really very serious, that kids will be kids, and that the rough and tumble of the intensely competitive high school atmosphere prepares teenagers for survival in adult life. This point of view was expressed recently in a post-Columbine article in one of our leading news magazines. *Time* magazine visited a school where teachers were earnestly attempting to defuse some of the antagonism among various cliques and factions. The reporters seem to be mocking the efforts of these teachers by stating:

> So if you aren't allowed to wear a hat, toot your horn, form a clique, or pick on a freshman, all because everyone is worried that someone might snap, it's fair to ask: Are high schools preparing kids for the big ugly world outside those doors—or handicapping them once they get there? High school was once useful as a controlled environment, where it was safe to learn to handle rejection, competition, cruelty, charisma. Now that we've discovered how unsafe a school can be, it may have become so controlled that some lessons will just have to be learned elsewhere.

Here is one of our leading magazines expressing concern that if we mute the fierceness of daily competition just a bit, students may be deprived of the kind of experience that will prepare them for the harshly competitive "real" world outside. That strikes me as being akin to a 350-pound man worrying that using an artificial sweetener in his morning coffee might make him too thin. In other words, I am convinced there is plenty of competition and cruelty in an adolescent's world without our going out of our way to promote it at school. My concern is that most school administrators may not fully understand the profound effect that a hostile, competitive social environment can have on the development of student groups and their attitude toward each other.

As a social psychologist, I know that if the environment were a bit friendlier, a bit more cooperative, then youngsters would benefit enormously and would learn to appreciate one another to a greater extent than they now do. How do I know? Let me tell you about a simple little experiment performed in the woods some forty years ago. Muzafer Sherif, a distinguished social psychologist, wanted to see whether he could overcome an atmosphere of intense animosity that existed between two groups of boys at a summer camp. Toward this end, he and his colleagues conducted a rather diabolical little experiment that has become a classic in social psychology. I call the experiment "diabolical" because the researchers first had to go out of their way to create animosity between the two groups in order to set up the proper conditions for the experiment.

When the youngsters first arrived at the summer camp, Sherif assigned them to one of two groups—the Eagles or the Rattlers. He then set up a series of competitive activities in which the two groups were pitted against each other in a variety of games such as football, baseball, and tug-of-war. These competitive games built some cohesiveness within each group and some feelings of distance and rivalry between the two groups.

Capitalizing on these negative feelings, the researchers proceeded to intensify them by creating a number of situations in which they could treat one group like an in-group and the other like an out-group. For example, in one incident they arranged a camp party to which the Eagles were invited to come somewhat earlier than the Rattlers. The refreshments at the party consisted of two vastly different kinds of food: Half the food was fresh, appealing, and appetizing; the other half was stale, squashed, ugly, and unappetizing. Boys being boys, the early-arriving Eagles made a beeline for the most appetizing refreshments and loaded up their plates, leaving only the less interesting, less appetizing, stale, squashed, and ugly food for their adversaries. When the Rattlers arrived and saw how they had been taken advantage of, they were understandably annoyed—so annoyed they began to call the exploitive group rather uncomplimentary names. The Eagles, believing they deserved what they got (first come, first served), resented this treatment and responded in kind. Name-calling escalated into food throwing, and within a very short time a full-scale riot was in progress.

Following these incidents, the researchers tried to reverse the ill feeling they had caused. They began by eliminating the competitive games and by treating the two groups equally well. But this did no good at all. Once this level of hostility had been aroused, simply eliminating the factors that had originally aroused it did nothing to reduce it. On the contrary, even though there was nothing happening to generate hostility, the bad feelings continued to escalate. For example, when the two groups were engaged in such benign activities as sitting around watching movies, trouble was apt to break out.

Eventually, the researchers did find a way to reduce the hostility. They accomplished this by placing the two groups of boys in situations that required them to work with each other harmoniously—situations in which they had to cooperate with each other in order to accomplish a goal that was beneficial to all. For example, the researchers set up an emergency situation by intentionally damaging the water-supply system. The only way the system could be repaired was if all the youngsters worked together in a cooperative manner. On another occasion, the camp truck broke down while the boys were on a camping trip. In order to get the truck going again, it was necessary to push and pull it up a hill. The truck was heavy and the hill was steep; thus, they could attain their goal only if every single one of the youngsters worked together—regardless of whether they were Eagles or Rattlers. After several incidents of this kind there was a gradual diminution of hostile feelings.

Here is the lesson for schools: Hostility between groups can form and become entrenched very easily. Signs of favoritism toward one group and other types of perceived unfairness can increase inter-group antagonism. If schools want to decrease the animosity among cliques, repressing them is not enough. Schools have to offer students a common goal that they can all work toward together, within a structure that supports a positive sense of belonging.

We all know of instances where this kind of event happens spontaneously—without being planned or manipulated by diabolical experimenters. For example, when there is a natural disaster like a hurricane or a flood, neighbors frequently pitch in and help each other out. As a result of this experience, occasionally people who previously had little use for each other may come to feel closer to one another. Occasionally this kind of event comes about in dramatic fashion—even among sworn enemies.

In the summer of 1999, a devastating earthquake struck Turkey, taking the lives of some 30,000 people. In the immediate aftermath of the quake, hundreds of people were trapped under the rubble, hovering between life and death. Among the first foreigners on the scene were trained rescuers from the neighboring country of Greece. As you probably know, the Greeks and the Turks have been bitter enemies since the days of the Ottoman Empire, engaging in one conflict after another for centuries. The sight, on television, of Greeks helping clear away the rubble in order to rescue Turks had a salutary effect upon the feelings of both the Turks and the Greeks for one another.

A few weeks later, in a twist of fate that was so incredibly ironic it seems like it could only have been concocted in

Hollywood, an earthquake struck Greece. Turks immediately entered Athens to help with the rescue efforts. Here is the account that appeared in *The New York Times*:

> The day after Athens was struck by its most serious earthquake in decades, millions of television viewers throughout Greece watched in awe as Turkish rescue workers pulled a Greek child from under a pile of rubble. Announcers struggled to control their emotion. "It's the Turks!" one of them shouted as his voice began to crack. "They've got the little boy. They've saved him. And now the Turkish guy is drinking from a bottle of water. It's the same bottle the Greek rescuers just drank from. This is love. It's so beautiful."

A prominent American diplomat referred to this incident as "seismic diplomacy." These events were dramatic, meaningful, and heartwarming. They did, indeed, help to thaw ancient feelings of animosity and set the stage for a number of subsequent diplomatic overtures by both sides. But it would be naive to suggest that one or two incidents of friendly cooperation and helpfulness—no matter how dramatic—could succeed in overcoming centuries (or even months!) of hatred and distrust. Whether we are dealing with nations in conflict or students sitting in a classroom, isolated positive events, no matter how dramatic or heartwarming, cannot possibly overcome centuries, years, or even months of distrust and suspicion. If we want to create an atmosphere that promotes and sustains friendly feelings among diverse people, then we must find some way to build these positive cooperative experiences into their day-to-day activities. We must find a way to make friendly, co-operative encounters routine so that the resulting good feelings are bolstered. It is a challenge that we will explore in the next chapter.

6

ROOT CAUSE INTERVENTIONS, PART 2

Building Cooperation, Empathy, and Compassion in the Classroom

In William Wharton's provocative novel *Birdy,* one of the protagonists, Alfonso, a Sergeant in the army, develops an instant dislike for an overweight enlisted man, a clerk typist named Ronsky. There are a great many things that Alfonso dislikes about Ronsky. At the top of his list is Ronsky's annoying habit of continually spitting. He spits all over his own desk, his typewriter, and anyone who happens to be in the vicinity. Alfonso cannot stand the guy and has fantasies of punching him out. Several weeks later, Alfonso learns that Ronsky had taken part in the Normandy invasion and had watched, in horror, as several of his buddies were cut down before they even had a chance to hit the beach. It seems that his constant spitting was a concrete manifestation of his attempt to get the bad taste out of his mouth. On learning this, Alfonso sees his former enemy in an entirely different light. He sighs with regret and says to himself: "Before you know it, if you're not careful, you can get to feeling for everybody and there's nobody left to hate."

Do you like your job? If you do, then you probably work in a place where the people involved like one another, work well together, are supportive of one another, and are respectful of one another's minor idiosyncrasies and different styles of working. You are in a working situation where you feel respected and feel like an important member of a team—no matter what your job is.

Let me put some meat on those bare bones, by going into detail in my description of a highly supportive hypothetical work environment: In this well-functioning office, the people who work closely with one another are attentive to and supportive of individual differences in ways of working. For example, your immediate coworkers know that, after a meeting, Ned likes to shut himself in his office to work alone for a while. On the other hand, you and Chris enjoy working out some bugs in the project over coffee in the cafeteria or while exercising in the company gym. Sue and Sandy say they get their best ideas on their noontime walk. When the team comes back together, everyone has something valuable to say. The boss is a straight-up guy, too. Even though he supervises close to a hundred employees, he knows your name and remembers that you like to play the banjo. He can be a tough taskmaster—sometimes a little too tough—but he listens well and is almost always fair.

There's some petty office politics, of course—that can hardly be avoided. But it's no big deal and doesn't keep you awake at night. Most people just ignore it. It helps a lot that the men and women at your company get along pretty well together. There is a little competitiveness and a little envy but, for the most part, people root for each other, cooperate with each other, and are pleased by the success of a colleague. People can relax and even occasionally make innocent jokes, and nobody minds. Most people are happily married or happily single; no one's on the prowl.

You enjoy the Friday casual day, when everyone knocks off work early for the company get-together with pizza and basketball. Some of the basketball players were varsity athletes in high school or college. They're still really good and still love to play, but there aren't any company sports heroes or anything dumb like that. Nobody lionizes them like they did in high school; here they're just regular guys. The superstars in your organization are the ones who come up with creative ideas and support others in developing their ideas; they are also the ones who land the big contracts or really shine at their jobs. You can see that they're on the fast track to upper management. But even if you're not one of them, you still feel good about your role because you are always aware that you have something important to contribute, and the success of the superstars enhances things for everyone.

When things aren't going so great at home, you can always count on your coworkers to give you a sense of perspective and cheer you up. Things have been tense at home since your loudmouthed brother-in-law came to visit; your daughter's hair is a different color every week; and your son says he wants to use all the money he saved from his summer job to buy a motorcycle. By contrast, work seems like a refuge, filled with "normal" people who understand how trying home life can be. And if you have a really serious problem, the company has professional counselors you can talk to.

Things aren't perfect. There is often a lot of pressure and too much unnecessary drudge work. Occasionally, it's hard to rip yourself out of bed early in the morning to go to work, but you know they'd miss you if you didn't show up. Even with the deadlines and the ridiculous paperwork, you feel good about your job. You feel comfortable; you know you belong there. And that makes all the difference.

Now try to imagine a truly unpleasant work environment—a work environment from hell. You and your coworkers are constantly competing against one another in order to impress management. When you come up with a good idea, you can feel a chill in the air; instead of congratulating you and supporting your idea, your coworkers seem annoyed that they hadn't come up with that idea themselves. When you screw up at a work assignment, your coworkers are quick to smirk; sometimes they tease you or taunt you. Although you always considered yourself a warm

and supportive person, after a few months in this environment, you even find yourself experiencing pangs of envy
when one of your associates does well and feelings of joy
when one of them commits a stupid blunder.

Within your office, there are a definite in-group and out-
group. Interestingly enough, people in the in-group are not
necessarily the most skillful, the hardest-working, or the
most productive workers. Indeed, the people in the out-
group may be very good at what they do, but they also tend
to be rather shy or awkward; they don't dress fashionably.
One is obese.

You are in neither the in-group nor the out-group, but
somewhere in between. When you go to eat in the company
cafeteria, you are always at a loss as to where to sit. You
wish you would feel welcome by the in-group members—
but you aren't. You don't want to associate with those in the
out-group out of fear that doing so might lower your status
in the office. You would like to be in the in-group, but it's
not clear how one accomplishes that. Some of your coworkers in the in-group are actually untalented at their jobs, but
they are good at things that strike you as irrelevant to the
work that needs doing: One is a good golfer; one is a good
basketball player; one is flirtatious and looks good in tight
sweaters. Even the boss seems to favor these colleagues.

Sound wacky? It is. In such an atmosphere, no business
could hope to retain its best employees—or succeed. But
that's precisely the way it is at most high schools. Do you
know of any high schools where the academically brightest

and most cooperative students are the ones who are invariably liked best by their peers, where members of the debating team or the philosophy club are generally held in higher esteem than members of the football team? Do you know of any high school where off-beat, idiosyncratic behavior is actively encouraged or even tolerated?

It is almost a cliché for us middle-aged people to sigh wistfully and say, "I wish I were young again," but I suspect that most of us are choosing not to remember many of the harsher aspects of our teenage existence. If push ever came to shove, very few of us would really want to go back to high school. Nobody wants to deal with the academic demands of six different teachers, the emotional turmoil of adolescent hormones, feelings of inferiority if you're not a jock, a superstar, or physically attractive, loneliness if you don't have your own tight group to hang with, plus coping with parents who "just don't get it" and may be unreasonable, unsupportive, or unsympathetic. It is no wonder that students often prefer their after-school job at a fast-food restaurant to studying Renaissance art or the physics of space flight. What is more rewarding about frying burgers than learning about art or astrophysics? As illustrated by the hypothetical example at the beginning of this chapter, a positive work environment, even at a fairly menial job, can offer far more than a negative school environment. As employees, young people often experience the kind of teamwork, camaraderie, and responsibility that is often missing at their school.

A truly positive work environment is as exciting for what it is not as for what it is. In a positive work environment, there is an absence of put-downs, taunting, and exclusion. People don't go around humiliating one another. No one gets lionized for irrelevant and unattainable (for the rest of us) attributes—like being a fast runner or having bulging muscles or bulging breasts. People are respected for who they are. Differences are not simply tolerated, they are celebrated.

REDUCING COMPETITION/
FOSTERING COOPERATION

What can schools do to make the classroom environment as appealing to young people as their after-school jobs? You can't do it by adding prayer in the classrooms or posting the Ten Commandments on the bulletin board. You can't do it by forcing kids to call their teachers "sir" and "ma'am." You can't do it even by adding wonderful classes on Renaissance art or medieval history—as valuable as these courses might be. The best way I know to accomplish this is to restructure students' academic experience. I'm not talking about the content of the courses, but about the atmosphere created by the process of learning. In many respects, how a topic is learned is more important than the content of what is learned.

There are many ways to convey information to students. The teacher can lecture on a topic like World War II. Or students can read the facts about World War II in a text-book. The teacher can assign students to do their own research in the library, or have students interview people who served in the military or lived through the war period in the United States, Europe, and Asia. The teacher might require students to work individually or in groups. Students might be required to take a test, write a term paper, or give a talk to demonstrate what they have learned. One could use the format of a quiz show where the teacher asks questions and the students show their quickness and mastery of the subject by raising their hands as soon as they know the answer.

Each of these methods of conveying information sends a different message to students. Teachers who lecture send the message that they are an expert source of information. Teachers who dispatch students to the library send the message that it is useful for students to become skillful researchers, as well as learn about the topic at hand. Teachers who require students to interview a war veteran convey the implicit message that not all important information is contained in books. Teachers who run their class like a competitive quiz show indicate that quickness as well as knowledge is important.

The point is that students learn something from the process (the manner in which the product is attained or communicated) even while they are focusing on the content of the assignment. If students are required to take lecture notes, read textbooks, raise their hands as soon as they know the answer, and take tests graded on a curve, then the academic environment is designed to encourage students to compete against each other. When the grades come out, some students are big winners, some big losers, and most fall in the nameless middle zone. Students who have six classes like this may come to see life as competition—outside the classroom as well as inside it.

That's the atmosphere in most classrooms in this country—separating winners from losers. Perhaps that is why most of us tend to treat losing like a contagious disease. Most youngsters want to keep as far away from it as possible. The winners and those in the middle ground try to differentiate themselves from the losers. They don't associate with them; they taunt them; they want the losers to just "get lost." But, unless they drop out of school, losers don't disappear. In most cases, they simply suffer in silence, retreating further and further from the mainstream. The more they are ignored or taunted, the further away they drift. On rare, but significant, occasions, they explode—doing serious damage to themselves or others.

Many schools have attempted to counteract the negative influences of excessive competition. It would be hard to find a preschool or elementary school that did not actively encourage children to share, work harmoniously with others, and behave respectfully and cooperatively. Many elementary schools now have students sit in small groups at tables, rather than in rows of individual desks. Many schools focus a lot of attention on children with academic or behavior problems, going out of their way to include them as full and valued members of the class.

On the other hand, it would be hard to find a high school or middle school that goes out of its way to demonstrate a high value on inclusion and cooperation among all students. It is true that some schools have attempted to reduce the competitive atmosphere in the academic arena by eliminating tracking, opening Advanced Placement classes to all students, and doing away with class rankings and valedictorians. But these attempts miss the mark. Indeed, many parents and students view these strategies as an empty exercise in political correctness that serves only to penalize serious students who work hard. After all, no one would seriously entertain the idea of randomly assigning students to the starting lineup of the school's varsity football team, or playing intramural sports without scores or team rankings.

Attempts to enforce cooperation in the classroom can also backfire if not carefully designed. Simply assigning students to work together in groups to produce a joint report does not guarantee true cooperation. Most often the group dynamics of an unstructured "cooperative" situation of this sort mirror the larger competitive classroom dynamic. The one or two most able or most motivated students put themselves forward to do most of the work, while simultaneously resenting the fact that they are carrying the load for the entire group. The less able or less motivated students end up doing little, learning little, and feeling inadequate. These so-called "cooperative groups" are cooperative in name only.

THE JIGSAW CLASSROOM

The problem with cooperative learning assignments is not that they don't work. It is that they need to be carefully structured to work as intended. One successful model, with a three-decade track record, is the jigsaw classroom. "Jigsaw" is a specific type of group learning experience that requires everyone's cooperative effort to produce the final product. Just as in a jigsaw puzzle, each piece—each student's part—is essential for the production and full understanding of the final product. If each student's part is essential, then each student is essential. That is precisely what makes this strategy so effective.

Here is how it works: The students in a history class, for example, are divided into small groups of five or six students each. Suppose their task is to learn about World War II. In one jigsaw group let us say that Sara is responsible for researching Hitler's rise to power in prewar Germany. Another member of the group, Steven, is assigned to cover concentration camps; Pedro is assigned Britain's role in the war; Melody is to research the contribution of the Soviet Union; Bill will handle Japan's entry into the war; Clara will read about the development of the atom bomb.

Eventually each student will come back to his or her jigsaw group and will try to present a vivid, interesting, well-organized report to the group. The situation is specifically structured so that the only access any member has to the other five assignments is by listening intently to the report of the person reciting. Thus, if Bill doesn't like Pedro, or if he thinks Sara is a nerd, if he heckles them, or tunes out while they are reporting, he cannot possibly do well on the test that follows.

In order to increase the probability that each report will be factual and accurate, the students doing the research do not immediately take it back to their jigsaw group. After doing their research, they must first meet with the other students (one from each of the jigsaw groups) who had the identical assignment. For example, those students assigned to the atom bomb topic will meet together to work as a team of specialists, gathering information, discussing ideas, becoming experts on their topic, and rehearsing their presentations. We call this the "expert" group. It is particularly useful for those students who might have initial difficulty learning or organizing their part of the assignment—for it allows them to benefit from paying attention to and rehearsing with other "experts," to pick up strategies of presentation, and generally to bring themselves up to speed.

After this meeting, when each presenter is up to speed, the jigsaw groups reconvene in their initial heterogeneous configuration. The atom bomb expert in each group teaches the other group members what she has learned about the development of the atom bomb. Each student in each group educates the whole group about his or her specialty. Students are then tested on what they have learned from their fellow group members about World War II.

What is the benefit of the jigsaw classroom? First and foremost, it is a remarkably efficient way to learn the material. But even more important, in terms of the present discussion, the jigsaw process encourages listening, engagement, and empathy by giving each member of the group an essential part to play in the academic activity. Group members must work together as a team to accomplish a common goal. Each person depends on all the others. No student can achieve his or her individual goal (learning the material, getting a good grade) unless everyone works together as a team. Group goals and individual goals complement and bolster each other. This "cooperation by design" facilitates interaction among all students in the class, leading them to value one another as contributors to their common task.

In 1971, it was my privilege to witness this process unfold in Austin, Texas, in the very first jigsaw classroom ever held. My graduate students and I invented the jigsaw strategy that year, as a matter of absolute necessity, to help defuse a highly explosive situation. The city's schools had recently been desegregated and, because Austin had always been residentially segregated, white youngsters, African-American youngsters, and Mexican-American youngsters found themselves in the same classrooms for the first time in their lives. Within a few weeks, long-standing suspicion, fear, distrust, and antipathy between groups produced an atmosphere of turmoil and hostility, exploding into inter-ethnic fistfights in corridors and schoolyards across the city. The school superintendent called me in to see if we could do anything to help students learn to get along with one another. After observing what was going on in classrooms for a few days, my students and I concluded that inter-group hostility was being exacerbated by the competitive environment of the classroom.

Let me explain. In every classroom we observed, the students worked individually and competed against one another for grades. Here is a description of a typical fifth-grade classroom that we observed:

> The teacher stands in front of the class, asks a question, and waits for the children to indicate that they know the answer. Most frequently, six to ten youngsters raise their hands. But they do not simply raise their hands, they lift themselves a few inches off their chairs and stretch their arms as high as they can in an attempt to attract the teacher's attention. To say they are eager to be called on is an incredible understatement. Several other students sit quietly with their eyes averted, as if trying to make themselves invisible. These are the ones who don't know the answer. Understandably, they are trying to avoid eye contact with the teacher because they do not want to be called on.

> When the teacher calls on one of the eager students, there are looks of disappointment, dismay,

and unhappiness on the faces of the other students who were avidly raising their hands but were not called on. If the selected student comes up with the right answer, the teacher smiles, nods approvingly, and goes on to the next question. This is a great reward for the child who happens to be called on. At the same time that the fortunate student is coming up with the right answer and being smiled upon by the teacher, an audible groan can be heard coming from the children who were striving to be called on but were ignored. It is obvious they are disappointed because they missed an opportunity to show the teacher how smart and quick they are. Perhaps they will get an opportunity next time. In the meantime, the students who didn't know the answer breathe a sigh of relief. They have escaped being humiliated this time.

The teacher may have started the school year with a determination to treat every student equally and encourage all of them to do their best, but the students quickly sorted themselves into different groups. The "winners" were the bright, eager, highly competitive students who fervently raised their hands, participated in discussions, and did well on tests. Understandably, the teacher felt gratified that these students responded to her teaching. She praised and encouraged them, continued to call on them, and depended on them to keep the class going at a high level and at a reasonable pace.

Then there were the "losers." At the beginning, the teacher called on them occasionally, but they almost invariably didn't know the answer, were too shy to speak, or couldn't speak English well. They seemed embarrassed to be in the spotlight; some of the other students made snide comments—sometimes under their breath, occasionally out loud. Because the schools in the poorer section of town were substandard, the African-American and the Mexican-American youngsters had received a poorer education prior to desegregation. Consequently, in Austin, it was frequently these students who were among the losers. This tended unfairly to confirm the unflattering stereotypes that the white kids had about minorities. They considered them stupid or lazy. The minority students also had preconceived notions about white kids—that they were pushy show-offs and teacher's pets. These stereotypes were also confirmed by the way most of the white students behaved in the competitive classroom.

After a while, the typical classroom teacher stopped trying to engage the students who weren't doing well. She felt it was kinder not to call on them and expose them to ridicule by the other students. In effect, she made a silent pact with the "losers"; she would leave them alone as long as they weren't disruptive. Without really meaning to, she gave up on these students, and so did the rest of the class. Without really meaning to, the teacher contributed to the difficulty the students were experiencing. After a while, these students tended to give up on themselves as well—

perhaps believing that they *were* stupid—because they sure weren't getting it.

It required only a few days of intensive observation and interviews for us to have a pretty good idea of what was going on in these classrooms. We realized that we needed to do something drastic to shift the emphasis from a relentlessly competitive atmosphere to a more cooperative one. It was in this context that we invented the jigsaw strategy. Our first intervention was with fifth-graders. First we helped several fifth-grade teachers devise a cooperative jigsaw structure for the students to learn about the life of Eleanor Roosevelt. We divided the students into small groups, diversified in terms of race, ethnicity, and gender, and made each student responsible for a certain portion of Roosevelt's biography. Needless to say, at least one or two of the students in each group were already viewed as "losers" by their classmates.

Carlos was one such student. Carlos was very shy and felt insecure in his new surroundings. English was his second language. He spoke it quite well, but with a slight accent. Try to imagine his experience: After attending an inadequately funded, substandard neighborhood school consisting entirely of Mexican-American students like himself, he was suddenly bused across town to the middle-class area of the city and catapulted into a class with Anglo students who spoke English fluently, seemed to know much more than he did about all the subjects taught in the school, and who were not reluctant to let him know it.

When we restructured the classroom so that students were now working together in small groups, this was terrifying to Carlos at first. He could no longer slink down in his chair and hide in the back of the room. The jigsaw structure made it necessary for him to speak up when it was his turn to recite. Carlos gained a little confidence by rehearsing with the others who were also studying Eleanor Roosevelt's work with the United Nations, but he was understandably reticent to speak when it was his turn to teach the students in his jigsaw group. He blushed, stammered, and had difficulty articulating the material that he had learned. Skilled in the ways of the competitive classroom, the other students were quick to pounce on Carlos's weakness and began to ridicule him.

One of my research assistants was observing that group and heard some members of Carlos's group make comments such as, "Aw, you don't know it, you're dumb, you're stupid. You don't know what you're doing. You can't even speak English." Instead of admonishing them to "be nice" or "try to cooperate," she made one simple but powerful statement. It went something like this: "Talking like that to Carlos might be fun for you to do, but it's not going to help you learn anything about what Eleanor Roosevelt accomplished at the United Nations—and the exam will be given in about fifteen minutes." What my assistant was doing was reminding the students that the situation had changed. The same behavior that might have been useful to them in the past, when they were competing against each other, was now going to cost them something very important: the chance to do well on the upcoming exam.

Needless to say, old dysfunctional habits do not die easily. But they do die. Within a few days of working with jigsaw, Carlos's groupmates gradually realized that they needed to change their tactics. It was no longer in their own best interest to rattle Carlos; he wasn't the enemy—he was on their team. They needed him to perform well in order to do well themselves. Instead of taunting him and putting him down, they started to gently ask him questions. The other students began to put themselves in Carlos's shoes so they could ask questions that didn't threaten him and would help him recite what he knew in a clear and understandable manner. After a week or two, most of Carlos's groupmates had developed into skillful interviewers, asking him relevant questions to elicit the vital information from him. They became more patient, figured out the most effective way to work with him, helped him out, and encouraged him. The more they encouraged Carlos, the more he was able to relax; the more he was able to relax, the quicker and more articulate he became. Carlos's groupmates began to see him in a new light. He became transformed in their minds from a "know-nothing loser who can't even speak English" to someone they could work with, someone they could appreciate, maybe even someone they could like. Moreover, Carlos began to see *himself* in a new light, as a competent, contributing member of the class who could work with others from different ethnic groups. His self-esteem grew and as it grew, his performance improved even more; and as his performance continued to improve, his groupmates continued to view him in a more and more favorable light.

Within a few weeks, the success of the jigsaw was obvious to the classroom teachers. They spontaneously told us of their great satisfaction about the way the atmosphere of their classrooms had been transformed. Adjunct visitors (such as music teachers and the like) were little short of amazed at the dramatically changed atmosphere in the classrooms. Needless to say, this was exciting to my graduate students and me. But, as scientists, we were not totally satisfied; we were seeking firmer, more objective evidence— and we got it. Because we had randomly introduced the jigsaw intervention into some classrooms and not others, we were able to compare the progress of the jigsaw students with that of the students in traditional classrooms in a precise, scientific manner. After only eight weeks there were clear differences, even though students spent only a small portion of their class time in jigsaw groups. When tested objectively, jigsaw students expressed significantly less prejudice and negative stereotyping, were more self-confident, and reported that they liked school better than children in traditional classrooms. Moreover, this self-report was bolstered by hard behavioral data: For example, the students in jigsaw classrooms were absent less often than those in traditional classrooms. In addition, academically, the poorer students in jigsaw classes showed enormous improvement over the course of eight weeks; they scored significantly higher on objective exams than the poorer students in traditional classes, while the good students continued to do well—as well as the good students in traditional classes.

COOPERATION: JIGSAW AND BASKETBALL

You might have noticed a rough similarity between the kind of cooperation that goes on in a jigsaw group and the kind of cooperation that is necessary for the smooth functioning of an athletic team. Take a basketball team, for example. If the team is to be successful, each player must play his or her role in a cooperative manner. If each player was hell-bent on being the highest scorer on the team, then each would shoot whenever the opportunity arose. In contrast, on a cooperative team, the idea is to pass the ball crisply until one player manages to break clear for a relatively easy shot. If I pass the ball to Sam, and Sam whips a pass to Harry, and Harry passes to Tony who breaks free for an easy layup, I am elated even though I did not receive credit for either a field goal or an assist. This is true cooperation.

As a result of this cooperation, athletic teams frequently build a cohesiveness that extends to their relationship off the court. They become friends because they have learned to count on one another. There is one difference between the outcome of a typical jigsaw group and that of a typical high school basketball team, however—and it is a crucial difference. In high school, athletes tend to hang out with each other and frequently exclude nonathletes from their circle of close friends. In short, the internal cohesiveness of an athletic team often goes along with the exclusion of everyone else.

In the jigsaw classroom, we circumvented this problem by the simple device of shuffling groups every eight weeks. Once a group of students was functioning well together, once the barriers had been broken down and the students showed a great deal of liking and empathy for one another, we would re-form the groupings. At first, the students would resist this re-forming of groups. Picture the scene: Debbie, Carlos, Tim, Patty, and Jacob have just gotten to know and appreciate one another and they are doing incredibly good work as a team. Why should they want to leave this warm, efficient, and cozy group to join a group of relative strangers?

Why, indeed? After spending a few weeks in the new group, the students invariably discover that the new people are just about as interesting, friendly, and wonderful as their former group. The new group is working well together and new friendships form. Then the students move on to their third group, and the same thing begins to happen. As they near the end of their time in the third group, it begins to dawn on most students that they didn't just luck out and land in groups with four or five terrific people. Rather, they realize that just about *everyone* they work with is a good human being. All they need to do is pay attention to each person, to try to understand him or her, and good things will emerge. That is a lesson well worth learning.

ENCOURAGING GENERAL EMPATHY

Students in the jigsaw classroom become adept at empathy. They come to understand students like Carlos with empathy. Empathy is what Bill Clinton is getting at when he utters that well-known phrase, "I feel your pain." When we watch a movie, empathy is what brings tears or joy in us when sad or happy things happen to a character. But why should we care about a character in a movie? We care because we have learned to feel and experience what that character experiences—as if it were happening to us. As infants and children, we experience empathy for members of our family and close friends. But most of us do not experience empathy for our sworn enemies. Thus, when watching an adventure movie such as *Star Wars,* most youngsters will cheer wildly when spaceships manned by members of the Evil Empire are blown to smithereens. Who cares what happens to Darth Vader's followers?

Is empathy a trait we are born with or is it something we learn? I believe we are born with the capacity to feel for another person. It is part of what makes us human. I also believe that empathy is a skill that can be enhanced with practice. If I am correct, then it should follow that working in jigsaw groups would lead to a sharpening of a youngster's general empathic ability because to do well in the group, the child needs to practice feeling what her groupmates feel. To test this notion, one of my graduate students, Diane Bridgeman, conducted a clever experiment in which she showed a series of cartoons to 10-year-old children. Half of the children had spent two months participating in jigsaw classes; the others had spent that time in traditional classrooms. In one series of cartoons, a little boy is looking sad as he waves good-bye to his father at the airport. In the next frame, a letter carrier delivers a package to the boy. When the boy opens the package and finds a toy airplane inside, he bursts into tears. Diane Bridgeman asked the children why they thought the little boy burst into tears at the sight of the airplane. Nearly all of the children could answer correctly—because the toy airplane reminded him of how much he missed his father. Then Diane asked the crucial question: "What did the letter carrier think when he saw the boy open the package and start to cry?"

Most children of this age make a consistent error; they assume that everyone knows what they know. Thus, the youngsters in the control group thought that the letter carrier would know the boy was sad because the gift reminded him of his father leaving. But the children who had participated in the jigsaw classroom responded differently. Because they were better able to take the perspective of the letter carrier—to put themselves in his shoes—they realized that he would be confused at seeing the boy cry over receiving a nice present because the letter carrier hadn't witnessed the farewell scene at the airport.

Offhand, this might not seem very important. After all, who cares whether kids have the ability to figure out what is in the letter carrier's mind? In point of fact, we should all care—a great deal. Here's why: The extent to which children can develop the ability to see the world from the perspective of another human being has profound implications for empathy, prejudice, aggression, and interpersonal relations in general. When you can feel another person's pain, when you can develop the ability to understand what that person is going through, it increases the probability that your heart will open to that person. Once your heart opens to another person, it becomes virtually impossible to bully that other person, to taunt that other person, to humiliate that other person—and certainly to kill that other person. If you develop the general ability to empathize, then your desire to bully or taunt *anyone* will decrease. Such is the power of empathy.

Recall that as a lead-in to this chapter, I quoted from the novel *Birdy* that touching statement by Alfonso: "Before you know it, if you're not careful, you can get to feeling for everybody and there's nobody left to hate." Yes, that is the power of the jigsaw method—it builds empathy among students who frequently disliked and distrusted one another and were motivated to reject, taunt, and fight with one another. After experiencing jigsaw for a couple of months, they literally ran out of people to hate.

WHAT DO THE STUDENTS SAY ABOUT JIGSAW?

Cooperative learning strategies are effective. Students learn the material as well as, or better than, students in traditional classrooms. We have almost thirty years of scientific research that clearly demonstrates this. The data also show that through cooperative learning the classroom becomes a positive social atmosphere where students learn to like and respect one another, and where taunting and bullying are sharply reduced. Students involved in jigsaw tell us that they enjoy school more and show us that they do by attending class more regularly. It goes without saying that the scientific results are important. But on a personal level, what is perhaps even more gratifying is to witness, firsthand, youngsters actually going through the transformation. Tormentors evolve into supportive helpers and anxious "losers" begin to enjoy learning and feel accepted for who they are. Occasionally, I am privileged to receive spontaneous, unsolicited letters from young men and young women who, many years earlier, had undergone such a transformation. To give you some of the flavor of this experience, I would like to share one such letter with you.

Dear Professor Aronson:

I am a senior at ———— University. Today I got a letter admitting me to the Harvard Law School. This may not seem odd to you, but let me tell you something. I am the sixth of seven children my parents had—and I am the only one who ever went to college, let alone graduate, or go to law school.

By now, you are probably wondering why this stranger is writing to you and bragging to you about his achievements. Actually, I'm not a stranger although we never met. You see, last year I was taking a course in social psychology and we were using a book you wrote called *The Social Animal,* and when I read about prejudice and jigsaw it all sounded very familiar—and then, I realized that I was in that very first class you ever did jigsaw in—when I was in the fifth grade. And as I read on, it dawned on me that I was the boy that you called Carlos. And then I remembered you when you first came to our classroom and how I was scared and how I hated school and how I was so stupid and didn't know anything. And you came in—it all came back to me when I read your book—you were very tall—about 6½ feet—and you had a big black beard and you were funny and made us all laugh.

And, most important, when we started to do work in jigsaw groups, I began to realize that I wasn't really that stupid. And the kids I thought were cruel and hostile became my friends and the teacher acted friendly and nice to me and I actually began to love school, and I began to love to learn things and now I'm about to go to Harvard Law School.

You must get a lot of letters like this but I decided to write anyway because let me tell you something. My mother tells me that when I was born I almost died. I was born at home and the cord was wrapped around my neck and the midwife gave

me mouth to mouth and saved my life. If she was
still alive, I would write to her too, to tell her that I
grew up smart and good and I'm going to law
school. But she died a few years ago. I'm writing to
you because, no less than her, you saved my life too.

Sincerely,
XXXX XXX

I think you will agree that it is a beautiful letter. For me,
it is just about the most moving letter I have ever received.
But when I read the signature I was startled to discover that
it did not belong to the boy that I had in mind—the boy who
in my previous writings I had referred to as "Carlos." The
young man who wrote me that lovely letter was mistaken.

I have a clear memory of sitting there with the letter in
my hand thinking about that young man and how wrong he
was. But after a few minutes, I fell into a reverie in which I
began to realize that perhaps that young man was not mistaken after all. That is, although I had a specific fifth-grader
in mind when I wrote about Carlos, there are a great many
children who come pretty close to fitting that description.
In my reverie, I began to grasp the implications of the possibility that there are thousands of youngsters all over
America who think they are Carlos. And, in the deepest possible way, they *are* all Carlos. Carlos is any child who has
been the unhappy recipient of put-downs, taunting, rejec-

tion, and loss of self-esteem—but who has managed to turn that around because the structure of the classroom changed, creating a different set of responses. To the child involved, it feels like a miracle. To the social psychologist, it is another vivid example of the power of the situation: What looks like a small, simple change in the structure of a social environment can have an enormous impact on the experience of the people in that environment.

WHO CAN BENEFIT FROM JIGSAW?

It is not just young children who can benefit from a cooperative learning experience. It can happen at all ages. A great many experiments have been done on young adults showing similar results to those we obtained with children. In one such experiment, college students were asked to interact with a person whom they believed to be a former mental patient. Because he was described as a former mental patient, the students were led to expect the person to behave in a rather weird manner. Some students were in a traditional learning situation with the "former mental patient," while others participated in a jigsaw group with this person. The results were striking: Those in the jigsaw group were quickly able to let go of their negative expectations; they liked the person better and enjoyed interacting with him more than those in the traditional setting. Students who went through the jigsaw session also described mental patients, in general, far more positively.

Ideally, it is best to bring people together in cooperative situations before strong animosities develop. I would recommend starting jigsaw in elementary school. To be most effective, jigsaw should be continued, at least for part of each school day, through high school. If I were building an ideal educational system in social psychological terms, I would use jigsaw for a large part of the school day from third grade (after children have developed adequate learning skills) through high school. But I am also realistic. There are other learning goals besides social psychological ones and learning strategies that are valuable for a variety of different reasons. Fortunately, jigsaw has powerful effects even if not used for the entire school day. Thus, speaking realistically, between grades three and six, I would use jigsaw for at least half the school day—building a firm basis of cooperation and empathy among the students. During middle school and high school, it would be reasonable to taper off a bit—being careful to make certain that jigsaw is never entirely eliminated from each student's daily experience.

WHAT MAKES JIGSAW SO EFFECTIVE?

When we work closely with other people in a cooperative venture, we must learn to pay attention to one another, to listen hard, and to try to figure out the best ways to communicate with each of the other people in our group. In the course of paying attention, we learn to take the perspective of the other person—to see the world the way he or she sees it. This inevitably builds empathy, compassion, and understanding.

There are other important elements in jigsaw that are absent from the usual competitive classroom atmosphere. One of the key aspects of jigsaw is that the group is striving together toward a common goal—just like the boys in the summer camp we discussed in Chapter 5. An added advantage of jigsaw—one that increases its impact—is that in these small groups each youngster enters the group bearing a unique gift. The gift is the segment of the lesson that he or she has learned. The only access that each of us has to Carlos's or Debbie's segment of the lesson is through Carlos or Debbie sharing that gift with us. Thus, jigsaw has an exchange of favors built into its very structure.

As we all know, when someone does us a favor or brings us a gift, it has a positive effect on our feelings for that person. That's axiomatic. It's so obvious, it hardly needs to be stated. What is less obvious is that it also works the other way around: Whenever we *do* a favor for another person, we undergo a surge of liking for that person. Can you guess why? It is part of the human tendency toward self-justification. Whenever we commit ourselves to a course of action, we try to justify that action. The way we treat a person—helping him or harming him—leads us to justify our treatment of that person, which, in turn, intensifies our feelings about that person. For example, if we caused pain to a person, we might feel bad about that. In order to reduce that bad feeling, we would try to justify that action by convincing ourselves that the victim deserved the harm we did him. Perhaps we will convince ourselves that he is a jerk or a vicious person who would have hurt us if we had given him the opportunity. This makes us feel better about our action, but it also sets the stage for doing even more harm in the future. Once we have decided that our victim is a terrible person who deserved the bad things that befell him, it becomes easier to hurt him again and again in the future. I call this "the escalation of aggression."

It is reasonably clear from the videotapes Harris and Klebold made that they nurtured the anger they felt toward their tormentors as a way of justifying the horrendous deed they were about to perform. "More rage, more rage! Keep building it on," Harris says. In a less drastic manner, one of the athletes who had tormented Harris and Klebold seems to be justifying his actions. Recall that in Chapter 4 this young man is quoted as saying of Harris and Klebold, "They were into witchcraft. They were into voodoo. Sure we teased them. But what do you expect with kids who come to school with weird hairdos and horns on their hats?"

The same dynamic can work in reverse: Whenever we exert effort on another person's behalf, we try to justify that effort by finding something about the person that convinces us that the good deed was worth doing. Thus, all other things being equal, we will like a person better *after* we have done him or her a favor in order to justify the effort we put out. In the past several years, research by social psychologists has proven that this phenomenon is very powerful. But clever people didn't need to wait for social psychologists for scientific proof. As far back as 1736, Benjamin Franklin made good use of this piece of wisdom as a political strategy—with great success. Franklin, disturbed by the political opposition and apparent animosity of a member of the Pennsylvania state legislature, set out to win him over:

> I did not aim at gaining his favour by paying any servile respect to him but, after some time, took this other method. Having heard that he had in his library a certain very scarce and curious book I wrote a note to him expressing my desire of perusing that book and requesting he would do me the favour of lending it to me for a few days. He sent it immediately and I returned it in about a week with another note expressing strongly my sense of the favour. When we next met in the House he spoke to me (which he had never done before), and with great civility; and he ever after manifested a readiness to serve me on all occasions, so that we became great friends and our friendship continued to his death. This is another instance of the truth of an old maxim I had learned, which says, "He that has once done you a kindness will be more ready to do you another than he whom you yourself have obliged."

COOPERATIVE LEARNING AS SELF-PERSUASION

In the years following the success of the jigsaw strategy, a few educational researchers developed slightly different alternative cooperative techniques. Like jigsaw, each of these techniques has been successful at enabling students to master their course work while building respectful relations among their peers, increasing their liking for school, and stimulating their motivation to learn. All of this is accomplished through a mechanism that I call self-persuasion. Our goal was to try to reduce the bigotry, suspicion, and negative racial stereotyping that was rampant among students in the Austin public school system. But we did not try to persuade students directly that bigotry is morally wrong. We did not present them with rational arguments aimed at showing them that African-Americans and Mexican-Americans are good, decent people who deserve to be respected. Neither did we declare "National Brotherhood Week." Such direct strategies have proven notoriously ineffective when it comes to changing emotional attitudes like those involved in prejudice or deep-seated attitudes of any kind. Rather, we placed students in a situation where the only way they could hope to perform well on the upcoming exam was by working with and listening to other students—even those against whom they were initially prejudiced. In the course of trying to do well for themselves, they came to appreciate the special qualities of the previously disliked youngsters. Self-interest may not be the prettiest of motives, but it is an opening. It succeeded in opening the door to a chain of behaviors and feelings that eventually produced open-mindedness and open-heartedness that was astonishingly beautiful to observe.

The reader will recall that Congress—in an attempt to prevent a recurrence of the Littleton massacre—passed a law making it legal for schools to post the Ten Commandments. I wish it were that simple. But anyone who knows anything about how the human mind works knows that posting the Ten Commandments would not do the trick. Students already know the Ten Commandments. Harris and Klebold were well aware of the commandment Thou shalt not kill. Tacking it up on the wall would not have deterred them from performing their outrageous action. Bullies already know that it's not considered nice to hurt someone smaller than themselves. The in-crowd in high school has already learned at home and through their religions that taunting, teasing, and humiliating less popular youngsters is not something that parents and parsons would approve of. Students know that it is not decent to spread ugly rumors about their fellow students or reveal their most personal secrets. Many do it anyway.

Again, let us return to the Columbine High School football player who admitted that he and his friends had teased and taunted Harris and Klebold. He made that statement without regret or remorse. Rather, he justified his behavior. He said:

> "Sure we teased them. But what do you expect with kids who come to school with weird hairdos and horns on their hats? It's not just jocks; the whole school's disgusted with them. They're a

bunch of homos, grabbing each other's private parts. If you want to get rid of someone, usually you tease 'em."

I can readily understand his discomfort with Harris and Klebold and I can empathize with it. How does a person deal with discomfort? The young man obviously believed that taunting, name-calling, and rejection were his only options. But what would have happened if the school had been able to show him a more humane option? From my experience conducting and observing jigsaw classrooms, I would be willing to bet you dollars to doughnuts that if this young man had spent a few weeks in a jigsaw group with Harris and Klebold, his attitude toward them (as well as their attitude toward him) would have been much more accepting. He would have been motivated to see their positive qualities. He would have found an alternative to taunting them. I cannot prove it, but based on some thirty years of experience with this technique, I am confident that, if the jigsaw strategy had been instituted a few years ago, Columbine High School would have been a happier place for all of its students and the tragedy could have been averted.

PROBLEMS WITH JIGSAW AND HOW TO OVERCOME THEM

The atmosphere of a cooperative classroom fosters the mutual respect that I have seen take place in scores of classrooms in all areas of this country. Moreover, the jigsaw has several additional advantages:

- Most teachers find jigsaw easy to learn.

- Most teachers enjoy working with it.

- It can be used in conjunction with other teaching strategies.

- It is effective even if only used for an hour or two per day.

- It is free for the taking.

Too good to be true? Well, yes and no. It would be misleading to suggest that the jigsaw sessions always go smoothly. There are always problems. Occasionally, a particularly dominant, active, or rambunctious student will attempt to do most of the talking in his or her group. How can we prevent that? There are always a few students who present behavior problems that can be disruptive to the functioning of a group. How does the teacher control those students if she is not physically present in that jigsaw group? Some students are poor readers or slow thinkers and might not be able to create an excellent report for their group. How can we help them? At the other end of the talent continuum, some students are so gifted that they might get bored working with students who aren't as quick or as talented as they are. What can be done about that? All of these problems are real, but not fatal. Here is how teachers have dealt with them successfully.

The Problem of the Dominant Student

Most jigsaw teachers have found it useful to appoint one of the students to be the discussion leader for each session, on a rotating basis. It is the leader's job to call on students in a fair manner and try to spread participation evenly. In addition, the students quickly realize that the group runs more efficiently and better progress is made if each student is allowed to present his or her material before questions are taken and comments are invited. The self-interest of the group will eventually reduce, and might even eliminate, the problem of dominance.

The Problem of the Slow Student

If a student has poor study skills, then he or she may bring an inferior report back to the jigsaw group and cause a diminished exam performance on the part of the rest of the group. If this were to happen, then the jigsaw experience might backfire. This would be akin to the untalented baseball player dropping a routine fly ball with the bases loaded, earning the wrath of his or her teammates.

The ideal solution is built into the jigsaw method; it is the expert group discussed earlier. To elaborate, each student is given time to read the material and to prepare an outline of a report. Before reciting that report to their jigsaw groups, all students enter an expert group consisting of the five or six students who have prepared a report on the same topic. In the expert group, the students have an opportunity to discuss their report and modify it based on the suggestions of the other members of their expert group. This system works very well. In the early stages, the teacher might want to monitor the workings of the expert groups carefully—just to make certain that every student ends with an accurate report to bring to his or her jigsaw group. Most teachers find that once the expert groups get the hang of it, close monitoring becomes unnecessary.

The Problem of Boredom and the Bright Student

What happens to the brightest students in the jigsaw situation? Don't they become impatient, bored, or resentful of the slower students? Boredom is not uncommon in any classroom, regardless of the techniques being used. No matter how gifted the teacher, how exciting the subject matter, how engrossing the activities, the classroom usually lacks the excitement, entertainment value, and pace of television or computer games.

Although it may be impossible to eliminate boredom from the school experience, teachers who have used the jigsaw technique report a great deal *less* boredom among their students than is the case in a more competitive classroom atmosphere. Our data support this observation: Students in jigsaw classes like school better than youngsters in the control classes. This is true for the bright students as well as the slower students.

But if jigsaw is not administered properly, the more gifted students will become bored. Gifted students might "get it" quicker than most of their groupmates. While one of the slower members of the group is reporting in a halting manner, one of the quicker members may have already grasped the general idea and may simply tune out and start looking out the window. There is an old adage, *docemur docendo* (he who teaches learns). In jigsaw groups, all students are encouraged to take on the mind-set of a teacher even when they are not actually reciting at the moment. This means paying close attention to the person reciting, looking for ways to encourage the reciter, or gently requesting additional clarification. This is an exciting change of pace for the students. It frees them from being passive receptacles of information and provides the opportunity to try new skills. This mind-set can transform what might have been a boring, impatient experience into an exciting challenge. Not only does this challenge produce psychological benefits, but the learning is frequently more thorough.

IF COOPERATIVE LEARNING IS SO GOOD, HOW COME EVERYONE DOESN'T USE IT?

Almost everyone believes that cooperation is a good thing. And even though jigsaw and other structured cooperative learning strategies have been utilized with great success by thousands of innovative teachers in classrooms across the country as well as in Europe, Asia, and the Middle East, the overwhelming majority of classroom teachers do not use these strategies. How come? I'm not sure. My best guess is that like everyone else, teachers do things in the way they were trained to do them; and most teachers have not been trained to use jigsaw. If teachers have heard about jigsaw, they may think it is difficult to learn and, understandably, may be feeling overburdened and overworked as it is, so why should they go out of their way to make a major change in their style of teaching?

Some teachers may feel that in this age of "back to basics" cooperative learning is simply a frill—aimed at improving the social life of students, not at getting youngsters to learn the basic material. This view is erroneous, however. Students in jigsaw classrooms perform as well as or better than students in traditional classrooms. Moreover, jigsaw is compatible with other learning strategies and is effective even if used for only one or two hours during the school day.

Some teachers may be reluctant to give up control of everything that goes on in their classrooms. To some teachers, what goes on in a jigsaw classroom might look chaotic—with several youngsters talking at once. To some teachers, anything that smacks of chaos should be avoided at all costs. But jigsaw is anything but chaotic. True, there are several youngsters talking at once—but at a given moment there is usually only one speaker in each group who is doing the talking. The others are almost always listening much more attentively than in the typical traditional classroom.

Some middle school or high school teachers may feel that it is too late. If youngsters have been in a competitive classroom situation for the first six years of their schooling, then introducing jigsaw during their last six years may simply not work. It is true that jigsaw has its strongest effect if introduced in elementary school. Children exposed to jigsaw in their early years of schooling need little more than a "booster shot" (one hour per day) of jigsaw in middle school and high school to thwart the epidemic of exclusion and taunting produced by the excessive competition in adolescent years.

But what if jigsaw has not been used in elementary school? Admittedly, it is an uphill battle to introduce cooperative learning to 16-year-olds who have never before experienced it. Old habits are not easy to break. But they can be broken. It is never too late to begin. It takes a bit longer, but most high school students participating in jigsaw groups for the first time show a remarkable ability to benefit from the cooperative structure.

Still other teachers may feel that they are already using some form of cooperative learning because they have occasionally placed their students in small groups, instructing them to cooperate. When they have done this, they are not exactly thrilled with the results. It should be clear to anyone who has read this book that cooperative learning requires more than seating youngsters around a table and telling them to share, to work together, to be nice to one another, and to cooperate. Such loose, unstructured situations do not contain the crucial elements and safeguards that make the jigsaw and other structured cooperative strategies work so well.

HOW CAN A TEACHER LEARN TO USE JIGSAW?

The jigsaw technique is easy to learn and cost-free. True, jigsaw is an invention—but it is neither patented nor copyrighted. I have intentionally placed it in the public domain because I want to give it away. It is free to whoever wants to use it. Detailed descriptions of the technique are available in scientific journals and in two other books I have written. A teacher or a school system does not need to buy anything—the books can be borrowed from libraries. (For exact references to these journals and books, see the references section at the back of this book.) Moreover, any classroom teachers who want to use jigsaw needs only to drop me a note on their school letterhead and I will be happy to send them the basic material on a floppy disk.

Other Cooperative Techniques

I'm pleased to report that the jigsaw technique is not the only cooperative game in town. The invention of jigsaw opened the door to a number of different cooperative learning strategies. Thus, teachers have a variety of techniques to choose from. Each of these strategies is unique, but they all have the same basic focus: In order to participate in the learning process, students must give up trying to triumph over their classmates and must learn to listen and share.

Sources where these strategies can be found are listed in the references section at the end of this book.

WHAT'S WRONG WITH COMPETITION, ANYWAY?

I cannot end this chapter without a clarification. Throughout my discussion, I have used terms like "excessive competition" to describe the goings-on in the typical American school. Don't get me wrong. I do not mean to imply that competition, in and of itself, is an evil. It is not. In our country, healthy competition has produced better mousetraps, motorcars, and microchips. It has also contributed to the development of gifted athletes capable of exceeding their personal best, as well as remarkably talented playwrights, dentists, musicians, scientists, and carpenters. There is nothing wrong with competition. But competition that is ruthless, relentless, and untempered by caring and cooperation establishes an atmosphere that is unpleasant, at best, and dangerous, at worst. In the sports arena, it breeds fans who cheer when the opposing quarterback is injured and jeer when their hero strikes out. In the classroom, it creates an atmosphere of winners and losers, of those few who are riding high at the center of things, and of those many who are standing alone and miserable—on the outside, looking in. I am not in favor of the elimination of competition. What I advocate is that competition be placed in the context of general cooperation and caring. My research has shown that such a context is remarkably easy to create and enormously beneficial.

7

SUMMARY AND CONCLUSIONS

IT AIN'T WHAT WE SAY THAT COUNTS, IT'S WHAT WE DO

> "Those who do not increase knowledge
> decrease knowledge.
> But don't mistake knowledge for talk.
> One who knows, acts knowingly.
> Fools talk, and their talk often fools."
>
> —HILLEL

Competition, exclusion, taunting, and humiliation are neither natural nor inevitable. These experiences are not necessarily part and parcel of being a teenager in high school—though it often seems that way. Twenty-five years of careful research by social psychologists demonstrates conclusively that we can do better than that. And we *must* do better than that. The poet W. H. Auden wrote: "We must love one another or die." That is a beautiful and powerful statement—but perhaps a bit *too* powerful. In my judgment, loving one another is very nice, but not essential. It is essential that we learn to respect one another and to feel empathy and compassion for one another—even for those who, on the surface, might seem very different from us in race, ethnicity, interests, athleticism, appearance, style of dress, and so on.

In Chapters 5 and 6, we suggested two different approaches to achieve this goal: developing emotional intelligence and learning academic subjects in the context of a cooperative classroom structure. What these two approaches have in common is what I call "experiential learning," or learning through direct experience. Students discover the humanity and the beauty of their classmates not because a teacher lectures them about the essential brotherhood of man or the importance of being nice to one's peers, but through their own actions and experiences. When students pay attention to one another, cooperate with one another, and share their knowledge with one another, they gain respect, understanding, and empathy for one another. What teachers say is not unimportant, it's just that—where interpersonal attitudes are concerned—what students discover about one another on their own, in the process of learning, is of far greater importance.

In my own experiments in classrooms from coast to coast, I have seen thousands of students learn compassion and empathy in this manner. The results of this research have become a basic tenet of social psychological wisdom:

Where important, life-changing attitudes are concerned, lecturing does not have much of an effect. You don't get students from diverse backgrounds to appreciate one another by telling them that prejudice and discrimination are bad things. You get them to appreciate one another by placing them in situations where they interact with one another in a structure designed to allow everyone's basic humanity to shine through.

SOCIAL LEARNING AND MODELING

It is not only what *students* do, it is important what we teachers do (not what we preach, but what we practice). Imagine for a moment that you are a high school social studies teacher and just as your class is about to begin Dave, one of your less promising students, suddenly says, "I've decided one thing, anyway. I don't want to be an American. As soon as I get the chance, I'm leaving."

How would you respond? I would guess that some of you might be annoyed at that statement. It sounds ungrateful, at the very least, and perhaps even angry or hostile. It certainly doesn't sound like a thoughtful, considered judgment—and, to some, it might even sound stupid. So, if you were that teacher, would you express your annoyance? Would you tell Dave that his statement wasn't very thoughtful? Would you attempt to talk him out of it? Or would you simply ignore the statement and go on with your lesson plan?

Educators Ted and Nancy Sizer describe the response of a talented teacher, Ms. Santos, who found herself in precisely that situation. Ms. Santos took Dave's comment very seriously and looked at him with interest and respect. First, she simply asked him why he felt that way. Dave responded by saying that Americans act as if they are so great—but in actuality we are not even a true democracy because there are so many poor people and most of them are black. Other countries handle that kind of situation in better ways. "I'll just go live in one of them."

"Do you have another country in mind, Dave?"

It turns out that Dave does have two or three countries in mind, but when he mentions them, some of the other students respond by bringing up specific problems in those countries. A lively and vigorous discussion ensues. Dave holds his own, but, as the discussion continues, he appears increasingly willing to listen to and to think about the views being expressed by some of the other students. Throughout most of this discussion, Ms. Santos does not take an active part, but sits still, leans forward, and listens attentively.

After a while, Ms. Santos asks, "Do you want to live in a country without problems?" Her tone is calm, but the question is provocative. She has directed her question to Dave, in the context of the discussion, but the question embraces all of the students. Several of them begin to address the implications of that question. The teacher then helps the students think through the potential value of living in a country that can be considered "a work in progress"; that is, a country where there is still important and worthwhile work to be done. The students are inspired. They begin to come up with examples of people who have taken up that challenge—the challenge of working to make the country a better place for all of its citizens: Eleanor Roosevelt, Martin Luther King, Jr., Cesar Chavez, and the like. After a while, Dave comes up with an example himself. His voice has taken on a tone of interest and excitement. He seems less anguished, less disillusioned, more hopeful.

By taking the time to deal with Dave's question, Ms. Santos departed from her lesson plan. Some might say that she "lost" some fifteen or twenty minutes of valuable class time. But I would argue that what she gained was far more valuable than what might have been lost. By responding to Dave in a challenging but nonpunitive manner, Ms. Santos was not only modeling effective teaching, she was also showing that she respected Dave and his ideas—even though she might disagree with those ideas.

Ted and Nancy Sizer titled their book *The Students Are Watching*. It is a most appropriate title. Our students are more tuned in to what we do than what we say. If what we say is at odds with what we do, then it has an especially powerful impact on our students. For example, if Ms. Santos had been preaching the importance of behaving in a respectful manner, but consistently failed to show respect for Dave or any of his classmates, it would be almost certain to instill feelings of hopelessness and cynicism in her students.

I read about Dave and Ms. Santos a few weeks after reading a report in my local newspaper about a law passed in Louisiana that makes it mandatory for students to address their male teachers as "sir" and their female teachers as "ma'am." The reason for the legislation: In the wake of the Columbine massacre, the state legislature wanted to induce the students of Louisiana to learn to respect their teachers as well as their fellow students.

The contrast between these two items is striking. As a social psychologist, I know that one cannot legislate respect. Forcing people to obey arbitrary rules almost never has a positive effect (beyond getting people to go through the motions of obeying the rules). If I held a loaded gun to your head and ordered you to say that you loved me, I could probably get you to say you loved me. But my guess is that my behavior would not get you to love me. Punishing people for noncompliance with a rule might make them more compliant but it will not encourage them to appreciate the thing they are being forced to do. Forcing people to say respectful words is no way to teach respect.

Even *rewarding* people for doing something will not render that action more attractive. If you give your son a big enough reward for mowing the lawn, then it will get him to mow the lawn, but it will not get him to enjoy the process of mowing lawns. By the same token, if you want your student, Steve, to recite the multiplication tables, rewards work very well. Gold stars, praise, high grades, and presents will serve as incentives that will get him to learn the material. But these rewards will not lead Steve to *enjoy* doing the multiplication tables. As an educator, I don't care a lot whether Steve loves his multiplication tables, I just want him to learn them.

So what's the big deal? Let's take it a step further. Suppose I offer Steve a reward for reading Shakespeare. No problem. By offering him the same kinds of incentives as I did for doing his multiplication tables, I can get him to read Shakespeare. But here is precisely why it *is* a big deal: As an educator, I *do* care whether or not Steve will enjoy reading Shakespeare. Indeed, that is my purpose for exposing him to that great master. Will Steve learn to love Shakespeare because of the rewards I showered on him for doing that reading? For a teacher, that question is vital.

Unfortunately, the answer is no. Rewarding a person for reading Shakespeare could even thwart any tendency he might have to like the reading itself. Several experiments by Edward Deci and his colleagues make this point very nicely. Offering rewards to individuals for performing a pleasant activity actually decreases the attractiveness of that activity.

In one experiment, for example, college students worked individually on an interesting puzzle for an hour. The next day, half the students were paid one dollar for each piece of the puzzle they completed. The other students worked on the puzzle as before, without pay. During a third session, neither group was paid. The question is: How much liking did each group have for the puzzle? The researchers measured this during a third session by allowing the students to do whatever they pleased in a free period. The results are clear and convincing: During the free period, the unrewarded group spent more of their own time playing with the puzzle than the rewarded group. For the rewarded group, their excitement about the puzzle faded when there weren't any more rewards. In short, the researchers made the puzzle less fun for the students by offering them a reward. They actually turned play into work. This result reminds me of a statement made by the great basketball player Bill Russell. Russell reminisced about how much he loved playing basketball in high school and college, but then, "The game lost some of its magical qualities for me once I thought seriously about playing for a living."

Let us apply these findings to the issue of showing respect. If you cannot teach respect by forcing youngsters to obey an arbitrary rule or by rewarding them, then what can you do? Ms. Santos has already given us the answer. One of the best ways to induce youngsters to do anything is by modeling that behavior. Recall the experiment in which children became more aggressive when they watched an adult express aggressiveness by smacking around an inflatable Bobo doll. The same phenomenon applies to the modeling of desirable behavior. If the Louisiana school system wants children to show respect to teachers and to other children, then all the teachers need to do is model this behavior.

SOCIAL PSYCHOLOGY AND PUBLIC POLICY

I have discussed the fact that our first impulse is to blame someone following a horrifying tragedy like the Columbine massacre. This impulse is understandable, but finger-pointing usually doesn't prevent future tragedies. To prevent future tragedies, we must try to understand the root causes of the disaster and come up with interventions that reflect this understanding.

Policy makers frequently rush in with half-baked solutions in their zeal to be seen as doing something. The solutions might seem sensible on the surface, but in reality they do not have much chance of working. This is what happened with the Louisiana state legislature. The attempt of Congress to address the problem by passing legislation that allows schools to post the Ten Commandments on bulletin boards has the same problems. This intervention may be politically expedient, but, as public policy, it is feeble. Please don't get me wrong; I am not opposed to the Ten Commandments. It is certainly a magnificent code of ethics. I simply believe that posting it on a school's bulletin board will have very little impact on the behavior of our students. Every student knows about the Ten Commandments. I'm reasonably certain that they could even recite the most relevant items on the list. They know they are not supposed to kill or steal. They know they are supposed to honor their fathers and their mothers. They probably even know they are not supposed to mention God's name in vain—although my guess is that few are certain what that one means. But being able to recite the Ten Commandments and living by the Ten Commandments are two very different things. Those students who already have a moral compass do not need to be reminded that one should not kill or steal. Those who do not have a moral compass will not be prevented from killing or stealing by seeing a piece of paper tacked to the wall.

This book wasn't only about Columbine. My aim was not simply to try to prevent pathological "losers" from killing their fellow students. Rather, it was to suggest ways to transform the atmosphere in our schools so that there would be no losers, so there would be no one left to hate. I have used decades of social psychological research and wisdom in an effort to provide parents and teachers with the tools to help our schools become more supportive and more compassionate places. And this can be done without sacrificing the basic academic material that students are supposed to learn. The interventions suggested in these pages might require a little more effort than posting the Ten Commandments or forcing students to mouth superficial words of respect, but they are easily doable. Any competent teacher can treat students with the kind of respect shown by Ms. Santos. Any competent teacher can bring about an improvement in her students' emotional intelligence. Any competent teacher can learn to use the jigsaw method in a matter of hours. The solutions are right there in front of us. As teachers, principals, parents, and concerned citizens, we must see to it that they are used.

REFERENCES

Chapter 1

page 7

Aderholt, R. quoted in Mitchell, A., & Bruni, F. (1999, June 18). Guns and schools: The overview; House vote deals a stinging defeat to gun controls. *The New York Times*.

pages 17–18

Aronson, E. (1978). *The jigsaw classroom*. Beverly Hills, CA: Sage.

Aronson, E., & Patnoe, S. (1997). *Cooperation in the classroom: The jigsaw method*. New York: Longman.

Aronson, E., & Bridgeman, D. (1979). Jigsaw groups and the desegregated classroom: In pursuit of common goals. *Personality and Social Psychology Bulletin*, 5, 438–446.

Aronson, E. & Goode, E. (1980). Training teachers to implement jigsaw learning: A manual for teachers. In S. Sharan,

P. Hare, C. Webb, R. Hertz-Lazarowitz (Eds.), *Cooperation in education*. Provo, UT: Brigham Young University Press.

page 20

Dewey, J. (1916). *Democracy and education*. New York: Macmillan.

Chapter 2

pages 21–22

Aronson, E. (1999). *The Social Animal* (8th ed.). New York: Worth/W. H. Freeman.

page 24

Ross, L., Amabile, T. M., & Steinmetz, J. L. (1977). Social roles, social control, and biases in social-perception processes. *Journal of Personality and Social Psychology*, 35, 485–494.

page 28

Milgram, S. (1963). Behavioral study of obedience. *Journal of Abnormal and Social Psychology*, 67, 371–378.

page 33

Jacobs, J. (1999, December 20). Evil, not rage, drove teen killers. *San Jose Mercury News*, p. 7B.

page 35

Wilgoren, J., & Johnson, D. (1999, April 23). Terror in Littleton: The suspects; Sketch of killers: Contradictions and confusion. *The New York Times*.

Misty, B., & L'Engle, M. (1999). *She said yes: The unlikely martyrdom of Cassie Bernall*. Farmington, PA: Plough Publishing.

page 39

Morse, J. (1999, October 25). 3:30 pm: Mental health: A week in the life of a high school, Webster Groves. *Time* magazine, 154 (17).

page 41

Fischhoff, B. (1975). Hindsight foresight: The effect of outcome knowledge on judgment under uncertainty. *Journal of Experimental Psychology: Human Perception and Performance*, 1, 288–299.

Fischhoff, B., & Beyth, R. (1975). "I knew it would happen": Remembered probabilities on once-future things. *Organizational Behavior and Human Performance*, 13, 1–16.

Chapter 3

page 45

Howe, G. (1972). *Man, environment and disease in Britain*. New York: Barnes & Noble.

pages 50–51

Tribe, L. & Amar, A. R. (1999, October 28). Well-regulated militias, and more. [Op. ed. article]. *The New York Times*.

page 51

Quindlen, A. (1999, November 1). The widows and the wounded. *Newsweek*.

page 55

Goldberg, C., & Connelly, M. (1999, October 20.) Poll finds decline in teen-age fear and violence. *The New York Times*.

page 57

Bandura, A., Ross, D., & Ross, S. (1961). Transmission of aggression through imitation of aggressive models. *Journal of Abnormal and Social Psychology*, 63, 575–582.

page 57

Bandura, A., Ross, D., & Ross, S. (1963). A comparative test of the status envy, social power, and secondary reinforcement theories of identificatory learning. *Journal of Abnormal and Social Psychology*, 67, 527–534.

Bandura, A., Ross, D., & Ross, S. (1963). Vicarious reinforcement and initiative learning. *Journal of Abnormal and Social Psychology*, 67, 601–607.

Huston, A., & Wright, J. (1996). Television and socialization of young children. In T. M. MacBeth (Ed.), *Tuning in to young viewers: Social science perspectives on television*. Thousand Oaks, CA: Sage.

Seppa, N. (1997). Children's TV remains steeped in violence. *APA Monitor*, 28, 36.

Cantor, J. Confronting children's fright responses to mass media. In D. Zillmann, J. Bryant, & A. C. Huston (Eds.), *Media, children, and the family: Social scientific, psychodynamic, and clinical perspectives*. Hillsdale, NJ: Erlbaum.

page 58

Signorelli, N., Gerber, G., & Morgan, M. (1995). Violence on television: The Cultural Indicators Project. *Journal of Broadcasting & Electronic Media*, 39 (2), 278–283.

Huesmann, L. R. (1982). Television violence and aggressive behavior. In D. Pearly, L. Bouthilet, & J. Lazar (Eds.), *Television and behavior: Vol. 2. Technical Reviews* (pp. 220–256). Washington, DC: National Institute of Mental Health.

Eron, L., Huesmann, L., Lefkowitz, M., & Walder, L. (1996). Does television violence cause aggression? In D. Greenberg (Ed.), *Criminal careers, Vol. 2. The international library of criminology criminal justice and penology*. Hanover, NH: Dartmouth.

page 60

Liebert, R., & Baron, R. (1972). Some immediate effects of televised violence on children's behavior. *Developmental Psychology*, 6, 469–475.

page 61

Josephson, W. D. (1987). Television violence and children's aggression: Testing the priming, social script, and disinhibition prediction. *Journal of Personality and Social Psychology*, 53, 882–890.

Anderson, C., & Dill, K. (1999). Video games and aggressive thoughts, feelings, and behavior in the laboratory and in life. *Journal of Personality and Social Psychology*, in press.

Cline, V. B., Croft, R. G., & Courrier, S. (1973). Desensitization of children to television violence. *Journal of Personality and Social Psychology*, 27, 360–365.

page 65

Banks, T., & Dabbs, J. M., Jr. (1996). Salivary testosterone and cortisol in delinquent and violent urban subculture. *Journal of Social Psychology*, 136 (1), 49–56.

Dabbs, J. M., Carr, T. S., Frady, R. L., & Riad, J. K. (1995). Testosterone, crime, and misbehavior among 692 male prison inmates. *Personality and Individual Differences*, 7, 269–275.

page 66

Goldberg, W., & Connelly, M. (1999, October 20). Poll finds decline in teen-age fear and violence. *The New York Times*.

Berger, K. (2000). *The developing person through childhood and adolescence*. New York: Worth.

Chapter 4

page 71

Gibbs, N., & Roche, T., (1999, December 20). The Columbine Tapes. *Time* magazine, 154 (25).

page 73

Berger, K. (2000). *The developing person through childhood and adolescence*. New York: Worth.

page 77

Gibbs, N. (1999, October 24). A week in the life of a high school, Webster Groves. *Time* magazine, 154 (17).

page 79

Lewin, T. (1999, May 2). Terror in Littleton: The teen-age culture; Arizona high school provides glimpse inside cliques. *The New York Times*.

page 80

Townsend, P. (1999, May 23). *Santa Cruz Sentinel*, p. 89.

pages 81–82

Harmon, A. (1999, April 24). Terror in Littleton: The outcasts; Theme song on the Internet: The pain of social ostracism. *The New York Times*.

page 83

Garbarino, J. (1999). *Lost boys: Why our sons turn violent and how we can save them*. New York: Free Press.

Garbarino, J. (1999, December 20). Some kids are orchids. *Time* magazine, 154 (25).

page 86

Gilligan, J. (1992). *Violence: Our deadly epidemic and its causes*. New York: Grosset/Putnam.

Chapter 5

page 90

Goldberg, C., & Connelly, M. (1999, October 20). Poll finds decline in teen-age fear and violence. *The New York Times*.

Garbarino, J. (1999). *Lost boys: Why our sons turn violent and how we can save them*. New York: Free Press.

page 92

Goleman, D. (1995). *Emotional intelligence*. New York: Bantam Doubleday Dell.

page 94

Gardner quoted in Goleman, D. (1995). *Emotional intelligence*. New York: Bantam Doubleday Dell, pages 41–42.

Mischel, W., Shoda, Y., & Rodriguez, M. (1992). Delay of gratification in children. In G. Loewenstein, J. Elster, et al. (Eds.). *Choice over time*. New York: Russell Sage Foundation.

page 95

Pawelkiewicz, W. M. (1981). A multivariate study of the effects of background, personality, cognitive and situational variables upon delay processes in kindergarten, second and third grade children. University of Connecticut. Dissertation Abstracts International.

pages 96–97

Eisenberg, N., Fabes, R., & Shea, C. (1989). Gender differences in empathy and prosocial moral reasoning: Empirical investigations. In M. Brabeck, et. al (Eds.).*Who cares?: Theory, research, and educational implications of the ethic of care*. New York: Praeger.

Goleman, D. (1995). *Emotional intelligence*. New York: Bantam Doubleday Dell.

Hanson, R. A., & Mullis, R. L. (1985). Age and gender differences in empathy and moral reasoning among adolescents. *Child Study Journal*, 15 (3), 181–188.

Lennon, R., & Eisenberg, N. (1987). Gender and age differences in empathy and sympathy. In N. Eisenberg, J. Strayer, et al. (Eds.). *Empathy and its development*. New York: Cambridge University Press.

Maccoby, E. E. (1998). *The two sexes: Growing up apart, coming together*. Cambridge, MA: Belknap Press/Harvard University Press.

Maccoby, E. E. (1995). The two sexes and their social systems. In P. Moen, G. H. Elder, Jr., et al. (Eds.). *Examining lives in context: Perspectives on the ecology of human development*. Washington, DC: American Psychological Association.

Maccoby, E. E., & Jacklin, C. (1974). *The psychology of sex differences*. Stanford, CA: Stanford University Press.

Pollack, W. (1998). *Real boys: Rescuing our sons from the myths of boyhood*. New York: Random House.

page 99

Report: Women less violent; Findings: Men commit majority of crimes, more serious offenses. *San Jose Mercury News*. December 6, 1999.

page 100

Garbarino, J. (1999). *Lost boys: Why our sons turn violent and how we can save them*. New York: Free Press.

pages 104–105

Olweus, D. (1997). Tackling peer victimization with a school-based intervention program. In D. Fry & K. Bjorkqvist

(Eds.), *Cultural variation in conflict resolution: Alternatives to violence*. Hillsdale, NJ: Erlbaum.

Olweus, D. (1996). Bullying at school: Knowledge base and an effective intervention program. In C. Ferris & T. Grisso (Eds.). *Understanding aggressive behavior in children*. New York, NY: New York Academy of Sciences.

Olweus, D. (1991). Bully/victim problems among schoolchildren: Basic facts and effects of a school-based intervention program. In D. Pepler & K. Rubin (Eds.). *The development and treatment of childhood aggression*. Hillsdale, NJ: Erlbaum.

pages 108–111

Goleman, D. (1995). *Emotional intelligence*. New York: Bantam Doubleday Dell.

page 114

Feynman, R. (1985). *"Surely you're joking, Mr. Feynman!" Adventures of a curious character*. (As told to Ralph Leighton; edited by Edward Hutchings.) New York: Norton.

pages 114–115

Feshbach, N. (1997). Empathy: The formative years—implications for clinical practice. In A. Bohart & L. Greenberg, et al. (Eds.). *Empathy reconsidered: New directions in psychotherapy*. Washington, DC: American Psychological Association.

Feshbach, N. (1989). Empathy training and prosocial behavior. In J. Groebel & R. Hinde, et al. (Eds.). *Aggression and war: Their biological and social bases*. Cambridge, UK: Cambridge University Press.

Feshbach, N., & Cohen, S. (1988). Training affects comprehension in young children: An experimental evaluation. *Journal of Applied Developmental Psychology*, 9 (2), 201–210.

page 116

Goleman, D. (1995). *Emotional intelligence*. New York: Bantam Doubleday Dell.

Sizer, T., & Sizer, N. (1999). *The students are watching*. Boston: Beacon Press.

page 117

Asher, S. R., & Rose, A.J. (1997). Promoting children's social-emotional adjustment with peers. In P. Salovey, D.J. Sluyter, et al. (Eds.), *Emotional development and emotional intelligence: Educational implications*. New York: Basic Books.

page 118

Gibbs, N. (1999, October 24). A week in the life of a high school: Webster Groves. *Time* magazine, 154 (17).

page 119

Sherif, M., Harvey, O. J., White, B. J., Hood, W., & Sherif, C. (1961). *Intergroup conflict and cooperation: The Robbers Cave experiment*. Norman, OK: University of Oklahoma Institute of Intergroup Relations.

page 123

Kinzer, S. (1999, September 13). A sudden friendship blossoms between Greece and Turkey. *The New York Times*.

Chapter 6

pages 125–126

Wharton, W. (1979). *Birdy*. New York: Knopf.

page 126

Pines, A., & Aronson, E. (1988). *Career burnout*. New York: Free Press.

pages 135–144

Aronson, E. (1978). *The jigsaw classroom*. Beverly Hills, CA: Sage.

Aronson , E., & Patnoe, S. (1997). *Cooperation in the class-room: The jigsaw method*. New York: Longman.

page 149

Wharton, W. (1979). *Birdy*. New York: Knopf.

page 153

Aronson, E. (1999). *The Social Animal*, 8th edition. New York: Worth/Freeman.

page 156

Gibbs, N., & Roche, T. (1999, December 20). The Columbine tapes. *Time* magazine, 154 (25).

Jecker, J., & Landy, D. (1969). Liking a person as a function of doing him a favor. *Human Relations*, 22, 371–378.

pages 156–157

Bigelow, J. (Ed.). (1916). *The autobiography of Benjamin Franklin*. New York: G. P. Putnam's Sons.

page 168

Desforges, D. M., Lord, C. G., Ramsey, S. L., Mason, J. A., Van Leeuwen, M. D., West, S. C., & Lepper, M. R. (1991). Effects of structured cooperative contact on changing negative attitudes towards stigmatized social groups. *Journal of Personality and Social Psychology*, 60, 531–544.

Qin, Z., Johnson, D. W., & Johnson, R. T. (1995). Cooperative versus competitive efforts and problem solving. *Review of Educational Research*, 65, 29–143.

Sharan, S., Hare, P., Webb, C., & Hertz-Lazarowitz, R. (1980). *Cooperation in education*. Provo, UT: Brigham Young University Press.

Slavin, R. (1996). Research on cooperative learning and achievement: What we know, what we need to know. *Contemporary Educational Psychology*, 21, 43–69.

Walker, I., & Crogan, M. (1998). Academic performance, prejudice, and the jigsaw classroom: New pieces to the puzzle. *Journal of Community and Applied Social Psychology*.

Chapter 7

page 172

Sizer, T., & Sizer, N. (1999). *The students are watching*. Boston: Beacon Press.

page 175

Deci, E. (1971). Effects of externally mediated rewards on intrinsic motivation. *Journal of Personality and Social Psychology*, 18, 105–115.

Lepper, M. R., & Greene, D. (1975). Turning play into work: Effects of adult surveillance and extrinsic rewards on children's intrinsic motivation. *Journal of Personality and Social Psychology*, 31, 479–486.

page 176

Russell, B., & Branch, T. (1979). *Second wind: The memoirs of an opinionated man*. New York: Ballantine.

page 176

Bandura, A., Ross, D., & Ross, S. (1961). Transmission of aggression through imitation of aggressive models. *Journal of Abnormal and Social Psychology*, 63, 575–582.

WEB RESOURCES

The following are some sites on the Internet dealing with violence in schools with ideas for prevention.

Center for the Prevention of School Violence
20 Enterprise St., Ste 2
Raleigh, NC 27607-7375
Tel: 800-299-6054 or 919-515-9397
Fax: 919-515-9561
www.ncsu.edu

National School Safety Center
141 Dusenberg Dr., Ste 11
Westlake Village, CA 91362
Tel: 805-373-9977
Fax: 805-373-9277
www.nssc1.org

Connect for Kids
The Benton Foundation
950 18th Street, N.W.
Washington, DC 20006
Tel: 202-638-5770
Fax: 202-638-5771
www.connectforkids.org

Stop School Violence
This site has links to
many topics of interest
on the Web.
www.stopschoolviolence.com